Monologium

By

St. Anselm

Translated By

James Gardiner Vose

ANSELM'S MONOLOGIUM

ON THE BEING OF GOD

PREFACE.

In this book Anselm discusses, under the form of a meditation, the Being of God, basing his argument not on the authority of Scripture, but on the force of reason. It contains nothing that is inconsistent with the writings of the Holy Fathers, and especially nothing that is inconsistent with those of St. Augustine. --The Greek terminology is employed in Chapter LXXVIII., where it is stated that the Trinity may be said to consist of three substances, that is, three persons.

CERTAIN brethren have often and earnestly entreated me to put in writing some thoughts that I had offered them in familiar conversation, regarding meditation on the Being of God, and on some other topics connected with this subject, under the form of a meditation on these themes. It is in accordance with their wish, rather than with my ability, that they have prescribed such a form for the writing of this meditation; in order that nothing in Scripture should be urged on the authority of Scripture itself, but that whatever the conclusion of independent investigation should declare to be true, should, in an unadorned style, with common proofs and with a simple argument, be briefly enforced by the cogency of reason, and plainly expounded in the light of truth. It was their wish also, that I should not disdain to meet such simple and almost foolish objections as occur to me.

This task I have long refused to undertake. And, reflecting on the matter, I have tried on many grounds to excuse myself; for the more they wanted this work to be adaptable to practical use, the more was what they enjoined on me difficult of execution. Overcome at last, however, both by the modest importunity of their entreaties and by the not contemptible sincerity of their zeal; and reluctant as I was because of the difficulty of my task and the weakness of my talent, I entered upon the work they asked for. But it is with pleasure inspired by their affection that, so far as I was able, I have prosecuted this work within the limits they set.

I was led to this undertaking in the hope that whatever I might accomplish would soon be overwhelmed with contempt, as by men disgusted with some worthless thing. For I know that in this book I have not so much satisfied those who entreated me, as put an end to the entreaties that followed me so urgently. Yet, somehow it fell out, contrary to my hope, that not only the brethren mentioned above, but several others, by making copies for their own use, condemned this writing to long remembrance. And, after frequent consideration, I have not been able to find that I have made in it any statement which is inconsistent with the writings of the Catholic Fathers, or especially with those of St. Augustine. Wherefore, if it shall appear to any man that I have offered in this work any thought that is either too novel or discordant with the truth, I ask him not to denounce me at once as one who boldly seizes upon new ideas, or as a maintainer of falsehood; but let him first read diligently Augustine's books on the Trinity, and then judge my treatise in the light of those.

In stating that the supreme Trinity may be said to consist of three substances, I have followed the Greeks, who acknowledge three substances in one Essence, in the same faith wherein we acknowledge three persons in one Substance. For they designate by the word *substance* that attribute of God which we designate by the word *person*.

Whatever I have said on that point, however, is put in the mouth of one debating and investigating in solitary reflection, questions to which he had given no attention before. And this method I knew to be in accordance with the wish of those whose request I was striving to fulfil. But it is my prayer and earnest entreaty, that if any shall wish to copy this work, he shall be careful to place this preface at the beginning of the book, before the body of the meditation itself. For I believe that one will be much helped in understanding the matter of this book, if he has taken note of the intention, and the method according to which it is discussed. It is my opinion, too, that one who has first seen this preface will not pronounce a rash judgment, if he shall find offered here any thought that is contrary to his own belief.

CHAPTER I.

There is a being which is best, and greatest, and highest of all existing beings.

IF any man, either from ignorance or unbelief, has no knowledge of the existence of one Nature which is highest of all existing beings, which is also sufficient to itself in its eternal blessedness, and which confers upon and effects in all other beings, through its omnipotent goodness, the very fact of their existence, and the fact that in any way their existence is good; and if he has no knowledge of many other things, which we necessarily believe regarding God and his creatures, he still believes that he can at least convince himself of these truths in great part, even if his mental powers are very ordinary, by the force of reason alone.

And, although he could do this in many ways, I shall adopt one which I consider easiest for such a man. For, since all desire to enjoy only those things which they suppose to be good, it is natural that this man should, at some time, turn his mind's eye to the examination of that cause by which these things are good, which he does not desire, except as he judges them to be good. So that, as reason leads the way and follows up these considerations, he advances rationally to those truths of which, without reason, he has no knowledge. And if, in this discussion, I use any argument which no greater authority adduces, I wish it to be received in this way: although, on the grounds that I shall see fit to adopt, the conclusion is reached as if necessarily, yet it is not, for this reason, said to be absolutely necessary, but merely that it can appear so for the time being.

It is easy, then, for one to say to himself: Since there are goods so innumerable, whose great diversity we experience by the bodily senses, and discern by our mental faculties, must we not believe that there is some one thing, through which all goods whatever are good? Or are they good one through one thing and another through another? To be sure, it is most certain and clear, for all who are willing to see, that whatsoever things are said to possess any attribute in such a way that in mutual comparison they may be said to possess it in greater, or less, or equal degree, are said to possess it by virtue of some fact, which is not understood to be one thing in one case and another in another, but to be the same in different cases, whether it is regarded as existing in these cases in equal or unequal degree. For, whatsoever things are said to be *just*, when compared one with another, whether equally, or more, or less, cannot be understood as just, except through the quality of *justness*, which is not one thing in one instance, and another in another.

Since it is certain, then, that all goods, if mutually compared, would prove either equally or unequally good, necessarily they are all good by virtue of something which is conceived of as the same in different goods, although sometimes they seem to be called good, the one by virtue of one thing, the other by virtue of another. For, apparently it is by virtue of one quality, that a horse is called *good*, because he is strong, and by virtue of another, that he is called *good*, because he is swift. For, though he seems to be called good by virtue of his strength, and good by virtue of his swiftness, yet swiftness and strength do not appear to be the same thing.

But if a horse, because he is strong and swift, is therefore good, how is it that a strong, swift robber is bad? Rather, then, just as a strong, swift robber is bad, because he is harmful, so a strong, swift horse is good, because he is useful. And, indeed, nothing is ordinarily regarded as good, except either for some utility -- as, for instance, safety is called good, and those things which promote safety --or for some honorable character -- as, for instance, beauty is reckoned to be good, and what promotes beauty.

But, since the reasoning which we have observed is in no wise refutable, necessarily, again, all things, whether useful or honorable, if they are truly good, are good through that same being through which all goods exist, whatever that being is. But who can doubt this very being, through which all goods exist, to be a great good? This must be, then, a good through itself, since ever other good is through it.

It follows, therefore, that all other goods are good through another being than that which they themselves are, and this being alone is good through itself. Hence, this alone is supremely good, which is alone good through itself. For it is supreme, in that it so surpasses other beings, that it is neither equalled nor excelled. But that which is supremely good is also supremely great. There is, therefore, some one being which is supremely good, and supremely great, that is, the highest of all existing beings.

CHAPTER II.

The same subject continued.

BUT, just as it has been proved that there is a being that is supremely good, since all goods are good through a single being, which is good through itself; so it is necessarily inferred that there is something supremely great, which is great through itself. But, I do not mean physically great, as a material object is great, but that which, the greater it is, is the better or the more worthy, -- wisdom, for instance. And since there can be nothing supremely great except what is supremely good, there must be a being that is greatest and best, i. e., the highest of all existing beings.

CHAPTER III.

There is a certain Nature through which whatever is exists, and which exists through itself, and is the highest of all existing beings.

THEREFORE, not only are all good things such through something that is one and the same, and all great things such through something that is one and the same; but whatever is, apparently exists through something that is one and the same. For, everything that is, exists either through something, or through nothing. But nothing exists through nothing. For it is altogether inconceivable that anything should not exist by virtue of something.

Whatever is, then, does not exist except through something. Since this is true, either there is one being, or there are more than one, through which all things that are exist. But if there are more than one, either these are themselves to be referred to some one being, through which they exist, or they exist separately, each through itself, or they exist mutually through one another.

But, if these beings exist through one being, then all things do not exist through more than one, but rather through that one being through which these exist.

If, however, these exist separately, each through itself, there is, at any rate, some power or property of existing through self (*existendi per se*), by which they are able to exist each through itself. But, there can be no doubt that, in that case, they exist through this very power, which is one, and through which they are able to exist, each through itself. More truly, then, do all things exist through this very being, which is one, than through these, which are more than one, which, without this one, cannot exist.

But that these beings exist mutually through one another, no reason can admit; since it is an irrational conception that anything should exist through a being on which it confers existence. For not even beings of a relative nature exist thus mutually, the one through the other. For, though the terms *master* and *servant* are used with mutual reference, and the men thus designated are mentioned as having mutual relations, yet they do not at all exist mutually, the one through the other, since these relations exist through the subjects to which they are referred.

Therefore, since truth altogether excludes the supposition that there are more beings than one, through which all things exist, that being, through which all exist, must be one. Since, then, all things that are exist through this one being, doubtless this one being exists through itself. Whatever things there are else then, exist through something other than themselves, and this alone through itself. But whatever exists through another is less than that, through which all things are, and which alone exists through itself. Therefore, that which exists through itself exists in the greatest degree of all things.

There is, then, some one being which alone exists in the greatest and the highest degree of all. But that which is greatest of all, and through which exists whatever is good or great, and, in short, whatever has any existence -- that must be supremely good, and supremely great, and the highest of all existing beings.

CHAPTER IV.

The same subject continued.

FURTHERMORE, if one observes the nature of things he perceives, whether he will or no, that not all are embraced in a single degree of dignity; but that certain among them are distinguished by inequality of degree. For, he who doubts that the horse is superior in its nature to wood, and man more excellent than the horse, assuredly does not deserve the name of man. Therefore, although it cannot be denied that some natures are superior to others, nevertheless reason convinces us that some nature is so preeminent among these, that it has no superior. For, if the distinction of degrees is infinite, so that there is among them no degree, than which no higher can be found, our course of reasoning reaches this conclusion: that the multitude of natures themselves is not limited by any bounds. But only an absurdly foolish man can fail to regard such a conclusion as absurdly foolish. There is, then, necessarily some nature which is so superior to some nature or natures, that there is none in comparison with which it is ranked as inferior.

Now, this. nature which is such, either is single, or there are more natures than one of this sort, and they are of equal degree.

But, if they are more than one and equal, since they cannot be equal through any diverse causes, but only through some cause which is one and the same, that one cause, through which they are equally so great, either is itself what they are, that is, the very essence of these natures; or else it is another than what they are.

But if it is nothing else than their very essence itself, just as they have not more than one essence, but a single essence, so they have not more than one nature, but a single nature. For I here understand *nature* as identical with *essence*.

If, however, that through which these natures are so great is another than that which they are, then, certainly, they are less than that through which they are so great. For, whatever is great through something else is less than that through which it is great. Therefore, they are not so great that there is nothing else greater than they.

But if, neither through what they are nor through anything other than themselves, can there be more such natures than one, than which nothing else shall be more excellent, then in no wise can there be more than one nature of this kind. We conclude, then, that there is some nature which is one and single, and which is so superior to others that it is inferior to none. But that which is such is the greatest and best of all existing beings. Hence, there is a certain nature which is the highest of all existing beings. This, however, it cannot be, unless it is what it is through itself, and all existing beings are what they are through it.

For since, as our reasoning showed us not long since, that which exists through itself, and through which all other things exist, is the highest of all existing beings; either conversely, that which is the highest exists through itself, and all others through it; or, there will be more than one supreme being. But it is manifest that there cannot be more than one supreme being. There is, therefore, a certain Nature, or Substance, or Essence, which is through itself good and great, and through itself is what it is; and through which exists whatever is truly good, or great, or has any existence at all; and which is the supreme good being, the supreme great being, being or subsisting as supreme, that is, the highest of all existing beings.

CHAPTER V.

Just as this Nature exists through itself, and other beings through it, so it derives existence from itself, and other beings from it.

Seeing, then, that the truth already discovered has been satisfactorily demonstrated, it is profitable to examine whether this Nature, and all things that have any existence, derive existence from no other source than it, just as they do not exist except through it.

But it is clear that one may say, that what derives existence from something exists through the same thing; and what exists through something also derives existence from it. For instance, what derives existence from matter, and exists through the artificer, may also be said to exist through matter, and to derive existence from the artificer, since it exists through both, and derives existence from both. That is, it is endowed with existence by both, although it exists through matter and from the artificer in another sense than that in which it exists through, and from, the artificer.

It follows, then, that just as all existing beings are what they are, through the supreme Nature, and as that Nature exists through itself, but other beings through another than themselves, so all existing beings derive existence from this supreme Nature. And therefore, this Nature derives existence from itself, but other beings from it.

CHAPTER VI.

This Nature was not brought into existence with the help of any external cause, yet it does not exist through nothing, or derive existence from nothing. --How existence through self, and derived from self, is conceivable.

SINCE the same meaning is not always attached to the phrase, "existence through" something, or, to the phrase, "existence derived from" something, very diligent inquiry must be made, in what way all existing beings exist through the supreme Nature, or derive existence from it. For, what exists through itself, and what exists through another, do not admit the same ground of existence. Let us first consider, separately, this supreme Nature, which exists through self; then these beings which exist through another.

Since it is evident, then, that this Nature is whatever it is, through itself, and all other beings are what they are, through it, how does it exist through itself? For, what is said to exist through anything apparently exists through an efficient agent, or through matter, or through some other external aid, as through some instrument. But, whatever exists in any of these three ways exists through another than itself, and is of later existence, and, in some sort, less than that through which it obtains existence.

But, in no wise does the supreme Nature exist through another, nor is it later or less than itself or anything else. Therefore, the supreme Nature could be created neither by itself, nor by another; nor could itself or an other be the matter whence it should be created; nor did it assist itself in any way; nor did anything assist it to be what it was not before.

What is to be inferred? For that which cannot have come into existence by any creative agent, or from any matter, or with any external aids, seems either to be nothing, or, if it has any existence, to exist through nothing, and derive existence from nothing. And although, in accordance with the observations I have already made, in the light of reason, regarding the supreme Substance, I should think such propositions could in no wise be true in the case of supreme Substance; yet, I would not neglect to give a connected demonstration of this matter.

For, seeing that this my meditation has suddenly brought me to an important and interesting point, I am unwilling to pass over carelessly even any simple or almost foolish objection that occurs to me, in my argument; in order that by leaving no ambiguity in my discussion up to this point, I may have the better assured strength to advance toward what follows; and in order that if, perchance, I shall wish to convince any one of the truth of my speculations, even one of the slower minds, through the removal of every obstacle, however slight, may acquiesce in what it finds here.

That this Nature, then, without which no nature exists, is nothing, is as false as it would be absurd to say that whatever is is nothing. And, moreover, it does not exist through nothing, because it is utterly inconceivable that what is something should exist through nothing. But, if in any way it derives existence from nothing, it does so through itself, or through another, or through nothing. But it is evident that in no wise does anything exist through nothing. If, then, in any way it derives existence from nothing, it does so either through itself or through another.

But nothing can, through itself, derive existence from nothing, because if anything derives existence from nothing, through something, then that through which it exists must exist before it. Seeing that this Being, then, does not exist before itself, by no means does it derive existence from itself.

But if it is supposed to have derived existence from some other nature, then it is not the supreme Nature, but some inferior one, nor is it what it is through itself, but through another.

Again: if this Nature derives existence from nothing, through something, that through which it exists was a great good, since it was the cause of good. But no good can be understood as existing before that good, without which nothing is good; and it is sufficiently clear that this good, without which there is no good, is the supreme Nature which is under discussion. Therefore, it is not even conceivable that this Nature was preceded by any being, through which it derived existence from nothing.

Hence, if it has any existence through nothing, or derives existence from nothing, there is no doubt that either, whatever it is, it does not exist through itself, or derive existence from itself, or else it is itself nothing. It is unnecessary to show that both these suppositions are false. The supreme Substance, then, does not exist through any efficient agent, and does not derive existence from any matter, and was not aided in being brought into existence by any external causes. Nevertheless, it by no means exists through nothing, or derives existence from nothing; since, through itself and from itself, it is whatever it is.

Finally, as to how it should be understood to exist through itself, and to derive existence from itself: it did not create itself, nor did it spring up as its own matter, nor did it in any way assist itself to become what it was not before, unless, haply, it seems best to conceive of this subject in the way in which one says that *the light lights* or is *lucent*, through and from itself. For, as are the mutual relations of *the light* and *to light* and *lucent* (*lux, lucere, lucens*), such are the relations of *essence,* and *to be* and *being,* that is, *existing* or *subsisting*. So the supreme *Being,* and *to be* in the highest degree, and *being* in the highest degree, bear much the same relations, one to another, as *the light* and *to light* and *lucent*.

CHAPTER VII.

In what way all other beings exist through this Nature and derive existence from it.

THERE now remains the discussion of that whole class of beings that exist through another, as to how they exist through the supreme Substance, whether because this Substance created them all, or because it was the material of all. For, there is no need to inquire whether all exist through it, for this reason, namely, that there being another creative agent, or another existing material, this supreme Substance has merely aided in bringing about the existence of all things: since it is inconsistent with what has already been shown, that whatever things are should exist secondarily, and not primarily, through it.

First, then, it seems to me, we ought to inquire whether that whole class of beings which exist through another derive existence from any material. But I do not doubt that all this solid world, with its parts, just as we see, consists of earth, water, fire, and air. These four elements, of course, can be conceived of without these forms which we see in actual objects, so that their formless, or even confused, nature appears to be the material of all bodies, distinguished by their own forms. -- I say that I do not doubt this. But I ask, whence this very material that I have mentioned, the material of the mundane mass, derives its existence. For, if there is some material of this material, then that is more truly the material of the physical universe.

If, then, the universe of things, whether visible or invisible, derives existence from any material, certainly it not only cannot be, but it cannot even be supposed to be, from any other material than from the supreme Nature or from itself, or from some third being -- but this last, at any rate, does not exist. For, indeed, nothing is even conceivable except that highest of all beings, which exists through itself, and the universe of beings which exist, not through themselves, but through this supreme Being. Hence, that which has no existence at all is not the material of anything.

From its own nature the universe cannot derive existence, since, if this were the case, it would in some sort exist through itself and so through another than that through which all things exist. But all these suppositions are false.

Again, everything that derives existence from material derives existence from another, and exists later than that other. Therefore, since nothing is other than itself, or later than itself, it follows that nothing derives material existence from itself.

But if, from the material of the supreme Nature itself, any lesser being can derive existence, the supreme good is subject to change and corruption. But this it is impious to suppose. Hence, since everything that is other than this supreme Nature is less than it, it is impossible that anything other than it in this way derives existence from it.

Furthermore: doubtless that is in no wise good, through which the supreme good is subjected to change or corruption. But, if any lesser nature derives existence from the material of the supreme good, inasmuch as nothing exists whencesoever, except through the supreme Being, the supreme good is subjected to change and corruption through the supreme Being itself. Hence, the supreme Being, which is itself the supreme good, is by no means good; which is a contradiction. There is, therefore, no lesser nature which derives existence in a material way from the supreme Nature.

Since, then, it is evident that the essence of those things which exist through another does not derive existence as if materially, from the supreme Essence, nor from itself, nor from another, it is manifest that it derives existence from no material. Hence, seeing that whatever is exists through the supreme Being, nor can anything else exist through this Being, except by its creation, or by its existence as material, it follows, necessarily, that nothing besides it exists, except by its creation. And, since nothing else is or has been, except that supreme Being and the beings created by it, it could create nothing at all through any other instrument or aid than itself. But all that it has created, it has doubtless created either from something, as from material, or from nothing.

Since, then, it is most patent that the essence of all beings, except the supreme Essence, was created by that supreme Essence, and derives existence from no material, doubtless nothing can be more clear than that this supreme Essence nevertheless produced from nothing, alone and through itself, the world of material things, so numerous a multitude, formed in such beauty, varied in such order, so fitly diversified.

CHAPTER VIII.

How it is to be understood that this Nature created all things from nothing.

BUT we are confronted with a doubt regarding this term *nothing*. For, from whatever source anything is created, that source is the cause of what is created from it, and, necessarily, every cause affords some assistance to the being of what it effects. This is so firmly believed, as a result of experience, by every one, that the belief can be wrested from no one by argument, and can scarcely be purloined by sophistry.

Accordingly, if anything was created from nothing, this very nothing was the cause of what was created from it. But how could that which had no existence, assist anything in coming into existence? If, however, no aid to the existence of anything ever had its source in nothing, who can be convinced, and how, that anything is created out of nothing?

Moreover, nothing either means something, or does not mean something. But if nothing is something, whatever has been created from nothing has been created from something. If, however, nothing is not something; since it is inconceivable that anything should be created from what does not exist, nothing is created from nothing; just as all agree that nothing comes from nothing. Whence, it evidently follows, that whatever is created is created from something; for it is created either from something or from nothing. Whether, then, nothing is something, or nothing is not something, it apparently follows, that whatever has been created was created from something.

But, if this is posited as a truth, then it is so posited in opposition to the whole argument propounded in the preceding chapter. Hence, since what was nothing will thus be something, that which was something in the highest degree will be nothing. For, from the discovery of a certain Substance existing in the greatest degree of all existing beings, my reasoning had brought me to this conclusion, that all other beings were so created by this Substance, that that from which they were created was nothing. Hence, if that from which they were created, which I supposed to be nothing, is something, whatever I supposed to have been ascertained regarding the supreme Being, is nothing.

What, then, is to be our understanding of the term *nothing?* -- For I have already determined not to neglect in this meditation any possible objection, even if it be almost foolish. --In three ways, then -- and this suffices for the removal of the present obstacle -- can the statement that any substance was created from nothing be explained.

There is one way, according to which we wish it to be understood, that what is said to have been created from nothing has not been created at all; just as, to one who asks regarding a dumb man, of what he speaks, the answer is given, "of nothing," that is, he does not speak at all. According to this interpretation, to one who enquires regarding the supreme Being, or regarding what never has existed and does not exist at all, as to whence it was created, the answer, "from nothing" may properly be given; that is, it never was created. But this answer is unintelligible in the case of any of those things that actually were created.

There is another interpretation which is, indeed, capable of supposition, but cannot be true; namely, that if anything is said to have been created from nothing, it was created from nothing itself (*de nihilo ipso*), that is, from what does not exist at all, as if this very nothing were some existent being, from which something could be created. But, since this is always false, as often as it is assumed an irreconcilable contradiction follows.

There is a third interpretation, according to which a thing is said to have been created from nothing, when we understand that it was indeed created, but that there is not anything whence it was created. Apparently it is said with a like meaning, when a man is afflicted without cause, that he is afflicted "over nothing."

If, then, the conclusion reached in the preceding chapter is understood in this sense, that with the exception of the supreme Being all things have been created by that Being from nothing, that is, not from anything; just as this conclusion consistently follows the preceding arguments, so, from it, nothing inconsistent is inferred; although it may be said, without inconsistency or any contradiction, that what has been created by the creative Substance was created from nothing, in the way that one frequently says a rich man has been made from a poor man, or that one has recovered health from sickness; that is, he who was poor before, is rich now, as he was not before; and he who was ill before, is well now, as he was not before.

In this way, then, we can understand, without inconsistency, the statement that the creative Being created all things from nothing, or that all were created through it from nothing; that is, those things which before were nothing, are now something. For, indeed, from the very word that we use, saying that it *created* them or that they were *created*, we understand that when this Being created them, it created something, and that when they were created, they were created only as something. For so, beholding a man of very lowly fortunes exalted with many riches and honors by some one, we say, "Lo, he has made that man out of nothing"; that is, the man who was before reputed as nothing is now, by virtue of that other's making, truly reckoned as something.

CHAPTER IX.

Those things which were created from nothing had an existence before their creation in the thought of the Creator.

BUT I seem to see a truth that compels me to distinguish carefully in what sense those things which were created may be said to have been nothing before their creation. For, in no wise can anything conceivably be created by any, unless there is, in the mind of the creative agent, some example, as it were, or (as is more fittingly supposed) some model, or likeness, or rule. It is evident, then, that before the world was created, it was in the thought of the supreme Nature, what, and of what sort, and how, it should be. Hence, although it is clear that the being that were created were nothing before their creation, to this extent, that they were not what they now are, nor was there anything whence they should be created, yet they were not nothing, so far as the creator's thought is concerned, through which, and according to which, they were created.

CHAPTER X.

This thought is a kind of expression of the objects created (*locutio rerum*), like the expression which an artisan forms in his mind for what he intends to make.

BUT this model of things, which preceded their creation in the thought of the creator, what else is it than a kind of expression of these things in his thought itself; just as when an artisan is about to make something after the manner of his craft, he first expresses it to himself through a concept? But by the *expression* of the mind or reason I mean, here, not the conception of words signifying the objects, but the general view in the mind, by the vision of conception, of the objects themselves, whether destined to be, or already existing.

For, from frequent usage, it is recognised that we can express the same object in three ways. For we express objects either by the sensible use of sensible signs, that is, signs which are perceptible to the bodily senses; or by thinking within ourselves insensibly of these signs which, when outwardly used, are sensible; or not by employing these signs, either sensibly or insensibly, but by expressing the things themselves inwardly in our mind, whether by the power of imagining material bodies or of understanding thought, according to the diversity of these objects themselves.

For I express a man in one way, when I signify him by pronouncing these words, a man; in another, when I think of the same words in silence; and in another, when the mind regards the man himself, either through the image of his body, or through the reason; through the image of his body, when the mind imagines his visible form; through the reason, however, when it thinks of his universal essence, which is a rational, mortal animal.

Now, the first two kinds of expression are in the language of one's race. But the words of that kind of expression, which I have put third and last, when they concern objects well known, are natural, and are the same among all nations. And, since all other words owe their invention to these, where these are, no other word is necessary for the recognition of an object, and where they cannot be, no other word is of any use for the description of an object.

For, without absurdity, they may also be said to be the truer, the more like they are to the objects to which they correspond, and the more expressively they signify these objects. For, with the exception of those objects, which we employ as their own names, in order to signify them, like certain sounds, the vowel a for instance -- with the exception of these, I say, no other word appears so similar to the object to which it is applied, or expresses it as does that likeness which is expressed by the vision of the mind thinking of the object itself.

This last, then, should be called the especially proper and primary *word*, corresponding to the thing. Hence, if no expression of any object whatever so nearly approaches the object as that expression which consists of this sort of *words,* nor can there be in the thought of any another word so like the object, whether destined to be, or already existing, not without reason it may be thought that such an expression of objects existed with (*apud*) the supreme Substance before their creation, that they might be created; and exists, now that they have been created, that they may be known through it.

CHAPTER XI.

The analogy, however, between the expression of the Creator and the expression of the artisan is very incomplete.

BUT, though it is most certain that the supreme Substance expressed, as it were, within itself the whole created world, which it established according to, and through, this same most profound expression, just as an artisan first conceives in his mind what he afterwards actually executes in accordance with his mental concept, yet I see that this analogy is very incomplete.

For the supreme Substance took absolutely nothing from any other source, whence it might either frame a model in itself, or make its creatures what they are; while the artisan is wholly unable to conceive in his imagination any bodily thing, except what he has in some way learned from external objects, whether all at once, or part by part; nor can he perform the work mentally conceived, if there is a lack of material, or of anything without which a work premeditated cannot be performed. For, though a man can, by meditation or representation, frame the idea of some sort of animal, such as has no existence; yet, by no means has he the power to do this, except by uniting in this idea the parts that he has gathered in his memory from objects known externally.

Hence, in this respect, these inner expressions of the works they are to create differ in the creative substance and in the artisan: that the former expression, without being taken or aided from any external source, but as first and sole cause, could suffice the Artificer for the performance of his work, while the latter is neither first, nor sole, nor sufficient, cause for the inception of the artisan's work. Therefore, whatever has been created through the former expression is only what it is through that expression, while whatever has been created through the latter would not exist at all, unless it were something that it is not through this expression itself.

CHAPTER XII.

This expression of the supreme Being is the supreme Being.

BUT since, as our reasoning shows, it is equally certain that whatever the supreme Substance created, it created through nothing other than itself; and whatever.it created, it created through its own most intimate expression, whether separately, by the utterance of separate words, or all at once, by the utterance of one word; what conclusion can be more evidently necessary, than that this expression of the supreme Being is no other than the supreme Being? Therefore, the consideration of this expression should not, in my opinion, be carelessly passed over. But before it can be discussed, I think some of the properties of this supreme Substance should be diligently and earnestly investigated.

CHAPTER XIII.

As all things were created through the supreme Being, so all live through it.

IT is certain, then, that through the supreme Nature whatever is not identical with it has been created. But no rational mind can doubt that all creatures live and continue to exist, so long as they do exist, by the sustenance afforded by that very Being through whose creative act they are endowed with the existence that they have. For, by a like course of reasoning to that by which it has been gathered that all existing beings exist through some one being, hence that being alone exists through itself, and others through another than themselves -- by a like course of reasoning, I say, it can be proved that whatever things live, live through some one being; hence that being alone lives through itself, and others through another than themselves.

But, since it cannot but be that those things which have been created live through another, and that by which they have been created lives through itself, necessarily, just as nothing has been created except through the creative, present Being, so nothing lives except through its preserving presence.

CHAPTER XIV.

This Being is in all things, and throughout all; and all derive existence from it and exist through and in it.

BUT if this is true -- rather, since this must be true, it follows that, where this Being is not, nothing is. It is, then, everywhere, and throughout all things, and in all. But seeing that it is manifestly absurd that as any created being can in no wise exceed the immeasurableness of what creates and cherishes it, so the creative and cherishing Being cannot, in anyway, exceed the sum of the things it has created; it is clear that this Being itself, is what supports and surpasses, includes and permeates all other things. If we unite this truth with the truths already discovered, we find it is this same Being which is in all and through all, and from which, and through which, and in which, all exist.

CHAPTER XV.

What can or cannot be stated concerning the substance of this Being.

NOT without reason I am now strongly impelled to inquire as earnestly as I am able, which of all the statements that may be made regarding anything is substantially applicable to this so wonderful Nature. For, though I should be surprised if, among the names or words by which we designate things created from nothing, any should be found that could worthily be applied to the Substance which is the creator of all; yet, we must try and see to what end reason will lead this investigation.

As to relative expressions, at any rate, no one can doubt that no such expression describes what is essential to that in regard to which it is relatively employed. Hence, if any relative predication is made regarding the supreme Nature, it is not significant of its substance.

Therefore, it is manifest that this very expression, that this Nature, is the *highest* of all beings, or *greater* than those which have been created by it; or any other relative term that can, in like manner, be applied to it, does not describe its natural essence.

For, if none of those things ever existed, in relation to which it is called *supreme* or *greater*, it would not be conceived as either *supreme* or *greater*, yet it would not, therefore, be less good, or suffer detriment to its essential greatness in any degree. And this truth is clearly seen from the fact that this Nature exists through no other than itself, whatever there be that is good or great. If, then, the supreme Nature can be so conceived of as not supreme, that still it shall be in no wise greater or less than when it is conceived of as the highest of all beings, it is manifest that the term *supreme*, taken by itself, does not describe that Being which is altogether greater and better than whatever is not what it is. But, what these considerations show regarding the term *supreme* or *highest* is found to be true, in like manner, of other similar, relative expressions.

Passing over these relative predications, then, since none of them taken by itself represents the essence of anything, let our attention be turned to the discussion of other kinds of predication.

Now, certainly if one diligently considers separately whatever there is that is not of a relative nature, either it is such that, *to be it* is in general better than *not to be it*, or such that, in some cases, *not to be it* is better than *to be it*. But I here understand the phrases, *to be it* and *not to be it*, in the same way in which I understand *to be true* and *not to be true*, *to be bodily* and *not to be bodily*, and the like. Indeed, to be anything is, in general, better than not to be it; as *to be wise* is better than *not to be so*; that is, it is better to be wise than not to be wise. For, though one who is just, but not wise, is apparently a better man than one who is wise, but not just, yet, taken by itself, it is not better *not to be wise* than *to be wise*. For, everything that is not wise, simply in so far as it is not wise, is less than what is wise, since everything that is not wise would be better if it were wise. In the same way, *to be true* is altogether better than *not to be so*, that is, better than *not to be true*; and *just* is better than *not just*; and *to live* than *not to live*.

But, in some cases, *not to be* a certain thing is better than *to be it*, as *not to be gold* may be better than *to be gold*. For it is better for man not to be gold, than to be gold; although it might be better for something to be gold, than not to be gold -- lead, for instance. For though both, namely, man and lead are not gold, man is something as much better than gold, as he would be of inferior nature, were he gold; while lead is something as much more base than gold, as it would be more precious, were it gold.

But, from the fact that the supreme Nature may be so conceived of as not supreme, that *supreme* is neither in general better than *not supreme*, nor *not supreme* better, in any case, than *supreme* -- from this fact it is evident that there are many relative expressions which are by no means included in this classification. Whether, however, any are so included, I refrain from inquiring; since it is sufficient, for my purpose, that undoubtedly none of these, taken by itself, describes the substance of the supreme Nature.

Since, then, it is true of whatever else there is, that, if it is taken independently, *to be it* is better than *not to be it*; as it is impious to suppose that the substance of the supreme Nature is anything, than which what is not it is in any way better, it must be true that this substance is whatever is, in general, better than what is not it. For, it alone is that, than which there is nothing better at all, and which is better than all things, which are not what it is.

It is not a material body, then, or any of those things which the bodily senses discern. For, then all these there is something better, which is not what they themselves are. For, the rational mind, as to which no bodily sense can perceive what, or of what character, or how great, it is --the less this rational mind would be if it were any of those things that are in the scope of the bodily senses, the greater it is than any of these. For by no means should this supreme Being be said to be any of those things to which something, which they themselves are not, is superior; and it should by all means, as our reasoning shows, be said to be any of those things to which everything, which is not what they themselves are, is inferior.

Hence, this Being must be living, wise, powerful, and all-powerful, true, just, blessed, eternal, and whatever, in like manner, is absolutely better than what is not it. Why, then, should we make any further inquiry as to what that supreme Nature is, if it is manifest which of all things it is, and which it is not?

CHAPTER XVI.

For this Being it is the same to be just that it is to be justice; and so with regard to attributes that can be expressed in the same way: and none of these shows of what character, or how great, but what this Being is.

BUT perhaps, when this Being is called just, or great, or anything like these, it is not shown what it is, but of what character, or how great it is. For every such term seems to be used with reference to quantity or magnitude; because everything that is just is so through justness, and so with other like cases, in the same way. Hence, the supreme Nature itself is not just, except through justness.

It seems, then, that by *participation* in this quality, that is, justness, the supremely good Substance is called just. But, if this is so, it is just through another, and not through itself. But this is contrary to the truth already established, that it is good, or great or whatever it is at all, through itself and not through another. So, if it is not just, except through justness, and cannot be just, except through itself, what can be more clear than that this Nature is itself justness? And, when it is said to be just through justness, it is the same as saying that it is just through itself. And, when it is said to be just through itself, nothing else is understood than that it is just through justness. Hence, if it is inquired what the supreme Nature, which is in question, is in itself, what truer answer can be given, than *Justness*?

We must observe, then, how we are to understand the statement, that the Nature which is itself justness is just. For, since a man cannot be justness, but can possess justness, we do not conceive of a just man as *being* justness, but as possessing justness. Since, on the other hand, it cannot properly be said of the supreme Nature that it possesses justness, but that it is justness, when it is called just it is properly conceived of as being justness, but not as possessing justness. Hence, if, when it is said to be justness, it is not said of what character it is, but *what* it is, it follows that, when it is called just, it is not said of what character it is, but what it is.

Therefore, seeing that it is the same to say of the supreme Being, that it is just and that it is justness; and, when it is said that it is justness, it is nothing else than saying that it is just; it makes no difference whether it is said to be justness or to be just. Hence, when one is asked regarding the supreme Nature, what it is, the answer, *Just*, is not less fitting than the answer, *Justness*. Moreover, what we see to have been proved in the case of justness, the intellect is compelled to acknowledge as true of all attributes which are similarly predicated of this supreme Nature. Whatever such attribute is predicated of it, then, it is shown, not of what character, or how great, but *what* it is.

But it is obvious that whatever good thing the supreme Nature is, it is in the highest degree. It is, therefore, supreme Being, supreme Justness, supreme Wisdom, supreme Truth, supreme Goodness, supreme Greatness, supreme Beauty, supreme Immortality, supreme Incorruptibility, supreme Immutability, supreme Blessedness, supreme Eternity, supreme Power, supreme Unity; which is nothing else than supremely being, supremely living, etc.

CHAPTER XVII.

It is simple in such a way that all things that can be said of its essence are one and the same in it: and nothing can be said of its substance except in terms of what it is.

Is it to be inferred, then, that if the supreme Nature is so many goods, it will therefore be compounded of more goods than one? Or is it true, rather, that there are not more goods than one, but a single good described by many names? For, everything which is composite requires for its subsistence the things of which it is compounded, and, indeed, owes to them the fact of its existence, because, whatever it is, it is through these things; and they are not what they are through it, and therefore it is not at all supreme. If, then, that Nature is compounded of more goods than one, all these facts that are true of every composite must be applicable to it. But this impious falsehood the whole cogency of the truth that was shown above refutes and overthrows, through a clear argument.

Since, then, that Nature is by no means composite and yet is by all means those so many goods, necessarily all these are not more than one, but are one. Any one of them is, therefore, the same as all, whether taken all at once or separately. Therefore, just as whatever is attributed to the essence of the supreme Substance is one; so this substance is whatever it is essentially in one way, and by virtue of one consideration. For, when a man is said to be a material body, and rational, and human, these three things are not said in one way, or in virtue of one consideration. For, in accordance with one fact, be is a material body; and in accordance with another, rational; and no one of these, taken by itself, is the whole of what man is.

That supreme Being, however, is by no means anything in such a way that it is not this same thing, according to another way, or another consideration; because, whatever it is essentially in any way, this is all of what it is. Therefore, nothing that is truly said of the supreme Being is accepted in terms of quality or quantity, but only in terms of *what* it is. For, whatever it is in terms of either quality or quantity would constitute still another element, in terms of what it is; hence, it would not be simple, but composite.

CHAPTER XVIII.

It is without beginning and without end.

FROM what time, then, as this so simple Nature which creates and animates all things existed, or until what time is it to exist? Or rather, let us ask neither from what time, nor to what time, it exists; but is it without beginning and without end? For, if it has a beginning, it has this either from or through itself, or from or through another, or from or through nothing.

But it is certain, according to truths already made plain, that in no wise does it derive existence from another, or from nothing; or exist through another, or through nothing. In no wise, therefore, has it had inception through or from another, or through or from nothing.

Moreover, it cannot have inception from or through itself, although it exists from and through itself. For it so exists from and through itself, that by no means is there one essence which exists from and through itself, and another through which, and from which, it exists. But, whatever begins to exist from or through something, is by no means identical with that from or through which it begins to exist. Therefore, the supreme Nature does not begin through or from, itself.

Seeing, then, that it has a beginning neither through nor from itself, and neither through nor from nothing, it assuredly has no beginning at all. But neither will it have an end. For, if it is to have end, it is not supremely immortal and supremely incorruptible. But we have proved that it is supremely immortal and supremely incorruptible. Therefore, it will not have an end.

Furthermore, if it is to have an end, it will perish either willingly or against its will. But certainly that is not a simple, unmixed good, at whose will the supreme good perishes. But this Being is itself the true and simple, unmixed good. Therefore, that very Being, which is certainly the supreme good, will not die of its own will. If, however, it is to perish against its will, it is not supremely powerful, or all-powerful. But cogent reasoning has asserted it to be powerful and all-powerful. Therefore, it will not die against its will. Hence, if neither with nor against its will the supreme Nature is to have an end, in no way will it have an end.

Again, if the supreme nature has an end or a beginning, it is not true eternity, which it has been irrefutably proved to be above.

Then, let him who can conceive of a time when this began to be true, or when it was not true, namely, that something was destined to be; or when this shall cease to be true, and shall not be true, namely, that something has existed. But, if neither of these suppositions is conceivable, and both these facts cannot exist without truth, it is impossible even to conceive that truth has either beginning or end. And then, if truth had a beginning, or shall have an end; before it began it was true that truth did not exist, and after it shall be ended it will be true that truth will not exist. Yet, anything that is *true* cannot exist without truth. Therefore, truth existed before truth existed, and truth will exist after truth shall be ended, which is a most contradictory conclusion. Whether, then, truth is said to have, or understood not to have, beginning or end, it cannot be limited by any beginning or end. Hence, the same follows as regards the supreme Nature, since it is itself the supreme Truth.

CHAPTER XIX.

In what sense nothing existed before or will exist after this Being.

BUT here we are again confronted by the term *nothing*, and whatever our reasoning thus far, with the concordant attestation of truth and necessity, has concluded nothing to be. For, if the propositions duly set forth above have been confirmed by the fortification of logically necessary truth, not anything existed before the supreme Being, nor will anything exist after it. Hence, nothing existed before, and nothing will exist after, it. For, either something or nothing must have preceded it; and either something or nothing must be destined to follow it.

But, he who says that nothing existed before it appears to make this statement, "that there was before it a time when nothing existed, and that there will be after it a time when nothing will exist." Therefore, when nothing existed, that Being did not exist, and when nothing shall exist, that Being will not exist. How is it, then, that it does not take inception from nothing or how is it that it will not come to nothing? -- if that Being did not yet exist, when nothing already existed; and the same Being shall no longer exist, when nothing shall still exist. Of what avail is so weighty a mass of arguments, if this *nothing* so easily demolishes their structure? For, if it is established that the supreme Being succeeds *nothing* [Nothing is here treated as an entity, supposed actually to precede the supreme Being in existence. The fallacy involved is shown below. --*Tr.*], which precedes it, and yields its place to *nothing*, which follows it, whatever has been posited as true above is necessarily unsettled by empty nothing.

But, rather ought this *nothing* to be resisted, lest so many structures of cogent reasoning be stormed by *nothing*; and the supreme good, which has been sought and found by the light of truth, be lost for *nothing*. Let it rather be declared, then, that nothing did not exist before the supreme Being, and that nothing will not exist after it, rather than that, when a place is given before or after it to nothing, that Being which through itself brought into existence what was nothing, should be reduced through nothing to nothing.

For this one assertion, namely, that nothing existed before the supreme Being, carries two meanings. For, one sense of this statement is that, before the supreme Being, there was a time when nothing was. But another understanding of the same statement is that, before the supreme Being, not anything existed. Just as, supposing I should say, "Nothing has taught me to fly," I could explain this assertion either in this way, that nothing, as an entity in itself, which signifies *not anything*, has taught me actually to fly -- which would be false; or in this way, that not anything has taught me to fly, which would be true.

The former interpretation, therefore, which is followed by the inconsistency discussed above, is rejected by all reasoning as false. But there remains the other interpretation, which unites in perfect consistency with the foregoing arguments, and which, from the force of their whole correlation, must be true.

Hence, the statement that nothing existed before that Being must be received in the latter sense. Nor should it be so explained, that it shall be understood that there was any time when that Being did not exist, and nothing did exist; but, so that it shall be understood that, before that Being, there was not anything. The same sort of double signification is found in the statement that nothing will exist after that Being.

If, then, this interpretation of the term *nothing*, that has been given, is carefully analysed, most truly neither something nor nothing preceded or will follow the supreme Being, and the conclusion is reached, that nothing existed before or will exist after it. Yet, the solidity of the truths already established is in no wise impaired by the emptiness of *nothing*.

CHAPTER XX.

It exists in every place and at every time.

BUT, although it has been concluded above that this creative Nature exists everywhere, and in all things, and through all; and from the fact that it neither began, nor will cease to be, it follows that it always has been, and is, and will be; yet, I perceive a certain secret murmur of contradiction which compels me to inquire more carefully where and when that Nature exists.

The supreme Being, then, exists either everywhere and always, or merely at some place and time, or nowhere and never: or, as I express it, either in every place and at every time, or finitely, in some place and at some time, or in no place and at no time.

But what can be more obviously contradictory, than that what exists most really and supremely exists nowhere and never? It is, therefore, false that it exists nowhere and never. Again, since there is no good, nor anything at all without it; if this Being itself exists nowhere or never, then nowhere or never is there any good, and nowhere and never is there anything at all. But there is no need to state that this is false. Hence, the former proposition is also false, that that Being exists nowhere and never.

It therefore exists finitely, at some time and place, or everywhere and always. But, if it exists finitely, at some place or time, there and then only, where and when it exists, can anything exist. Where and when it does not exist, moreover, there is no existence at all, because, without it, nothing exists. Whence it will follow, that there is some place and time where and when nothing at all exists. But seeing that this is false -- for place and time themselves are existing things -- the supreme Nature cannot exist finitely, at some place or time. But, if it is said that it of itself exists finitely, at some place and time, but that, through its power, it is wherever and whenever anything is, this is not true. For, since it is manifest that its power is nothing else than itself, by no means does its power exist without it.

Since, then, it does not exist finitely, at some place or time, it must exist everywhere and always, that is, in every place and at every time.

CHAPTER XXI.

It exists in no place or time.

BUT, if this is true, either it exists in every place and at every time, or else only a part of it so exists, the other part transcending every place and time.

But, if in part it exists, and in part does not exist, in every place and at every time, it has parts; which is false. It does not, therefore, exist everywhere and always in part.

But how does it exist as a whole, everywhere and always? For, either it is to be understood that it exists as a whole at once, in all places or at all times, and by parts in individual places and times; or, that it exists as a whole, in individual places and times as well.

But, if it exists by parts in individual places or times, it is not exempt from composition and division of parts; which has been found to be in a high degree alien to the supreme Nature. Hence, it does not so exist, as a whole, in all places and at all times that it exists by parts in individual places and times.

We are confronted, then, by the former alternative, that is, how the supreme Nature can exist, as a whole, in every individual place and time. This is doubtless impossible, unless it either exists at once or at different times in individual places or times. But, since the law of place and the law of time, the investigation of which it has hitherto been possible to prosecute in a single discussion, because they advanced on exactly the same lines, here separate one from another and seem to avoid debate, as if by evasion in diverse directions, let each be investigated independently in discussion directed on itself alone.

First, then, let us see whether the supreme Nature can exist, as a whole, in individual places, either at once in all, or at different times, in different places. Then, let us make the same inquiry regarding the times at which it can exist.

If, then, it exists as a whole in each individual place, then, for each individual place there is an individual whole. For, just as place is so distinguished from place that there are individual places, so that which exists as a whole, in one place, is so distinct from that which exists as a whole at the same time, in another place, that there are indiviual wholes. For, of what exists as a whole, in any place, there is no part that does not exist in that place. And that of which there is no part that does not exist in a given place, is no part of what exists at the same time outside this place.

What exists as a whole, then, in any place, is no part of what exists at the same time outside that place. But, of that of which no part exists outside any given place, no part exists, at the same time, in another place. How, then, can what exists as a whole, in any place, exist simultaneously, as a whole, in another place, if no part of it can at that time exist in another place?

Since, then, one whole cannot exist as a whole in different places at the same time, it follows that, for individual places, there are individual wholes, if anything is to exist as a whole in different individual places at once. Hence, if the supreme Nature exists as a whole, at one time, in every individual place, there are as many supreme Natures as there can be individual places; which it would be irrational to believe. Therefore, it does not exist, as a whole, at one time in individual places.

If, however, at different times it exists, as a whole, in individual places, then, when it is in one place, there is in the meantime no good and no existence in other places, since without it absolutely nothing exists. But the absurdity of this supposition is proved by the existence of places themselves, which are not nothing, but something. Therefore, the supreme Nature does not exist, as a whole, in individual places at different times.

But, if neither at the same time nor at different times does it exist, as a whole, in individual places, it is evident that it does not at all exist, as a whole, in each individual place. We must now examine, then, whether this supreme Nature exists, as a whole, at individual times, either simultaneously or at distinct times for individual times.

But, how can anything exist, as a whole, simultaneously, at individual times, if these times are not themselves simultaneous? But, if this Being exists, as a whole, separately and at distinct times for individual times, just as a man exists as a whole yesterday, to-day, and to-morrow; it is properly said that it was and is and will be. Its age, then, which is no other than its eternity, does not exist, as a whole, simultaneously, but it is distributed in parts according to the parts of time.

But its eternity is nothing else than itself. The supreme Being, then, will be divided into parts, according to the divisions of time. For, if its age is prolonged through periods of time, it has with this time present, past, and future. But what else is its age than its duration of existence, than its eternity? Since, then, its eternity is nothing else than its essence, as considerations set forth above irrefutably prove; if its eternity has past, present, and future, its essence also has, in consequence, past, present, and future.

But what is past is not present or future; and what is present is not past or future; and what is future is not past or present. How, then, shall that proposition be valid, which was proved with clear and logical cogency above, namely, that that supreme Nature is in no wise composite, but is supremely simple, supremely immutable? -- how shall this be so, if that Nature is one thing, at one time, and another, at another, and has parts distributed according to times? Or rather, if these earlier propositions are true, how can these latter be possible? By no means, then, is past or future attributable to the creative Being, either its age or its eternity. For why has it not a present, if it truly *is*? But *was* means past, and *will be* future. Therefore that Being never was, nor will be. Hence, it does not exist at distinct times, just as it does not exist, as a whole, simultaneously in different individual times.

If, then, as our discussion has proved, it neither so exists, as a whole, in all places or times that it exists, as a whole, at one time in all, or by parts in individual places and times; nor so that it exists, as a whole, in individual times and places, it is manifest that it does not in any way exist, as a whole, in every time or place.

And, since, in like manner, it has been demonstrated that it neither so exists in every time or place, that a part exists in every, and a part transcends every, place and time, it is impossible that it exists everywhere and always.

For, in no way can it be conceived to exist everywhere and always, except either as a whole or in part. But if it does not at all exist everywhere and always, it will exist either finitely in some place or time, or in none. But it has already been proved, that it cannot exist finitely, in any place or time. In no place or time, that is, nowhere and never does it exist. For it cannot exist, except in every or in some place or time.

But, on the other hand, since it is irrefutably established, not only that it exists through itself, and without beginning and without end, but that without it nothing anywhere or ever exists, it must exist everywhere and always.

CHAPTER XXII.

How it exists in every place and time, and in none.

How, then, shall these prepositions, that are so necessary according to our exposition, and so necessary according to our proof, be reconciled? Perhaps the supreme Nature exists in place and time in some such way, that it is not prevented from so existing simultaneously, as a whole, in different places or times, that there are not more wholes than one; and that its age, which does not exist, except as true eternity, is not distributed among past, present, and future.

For, to this law of space and time, nothing seems to be subject, except the beings which so exist in space or time that they do not transcend extent of space or duration of time. Hence, though of beings of this class it is with all truth asserted that one and the same whole cannot exist simultaneously, as a whole, in different places or times; in the case of those beings which are not of this class, no such conclusion is necessarily reached.

For it seems to be rightly said, that place is predicable only of objects whose magnitude place contains by including it, and includes by containing it; and that time is predicable only of objects whose duration time ends by measuring it, and measures by ending it. Hence, to any being, to whose spatial extent or duration no bound can be set, either by space or time, no place or time is properly attributed. For, seeing that place does not act upon it as place, nor time as time, it is not irrational to say, that no place is its place, and no time its time.

But, what evidently has no place or time is doubtless by no means compelled to submit to the law of place or time. No law of place or time, then, in any way governs any nature, which no place or time limits by some kind of restraint. But what rational consideration can by any course of reasoning fail to reach the conclusion, that the Substance which creates and is supreme among all beings, which must be alien to, and free from, the nature and law of all things which itself created from nothing, is limited by no restraint of space or time; since, more truly, its power, which is nothing else than its essence, contains and includes under itself all these things which it created? Is it not impudently foolish, too, to say either, that space circumscribes the magnitude of truth, or, that time measures its duration --truth, which regards no greatness or smallness of spatial or temporal extent at all?

Seeing, then, that this is the condition of place or time; that only whatever is limited by their bounds neither escapes the law of parts -- such as place follows, according to magnitude, or such as time submits to, according to duration -- nor can in any way be contained, as a whole, simultaneously by different places or times; but whatever is in no wise confined by the restraint of place or time, is not compelled by any law of places or times to multiplicity of parts, nor is it prevented from being present, as a whole and simultaneously, in more places or times than one -- seeing, I say, that this is the condition governing place or time, no doubt the supreme Substance, which is encompassed by no restraint of place or time, is bound by none of their laws.

Hence, since inevitable necessity requires that the supreme Being, as a whole, be lacking to no place or time, and no law of place or time prevents it from being simultaneously in every place or time; it must simultaneously present in every individual place or time. For, because it is present in one place, it is not therefore prevented from being present at the same time, and in like manner in this, or that other, place or time.

Nor, because it was, or is, or shall be, has any part of its eternity therefore vanished from the present, with the past, which no longer is; nor does it pass with the present, which is, for an instant; nor is it to come with the future, which is not yet.

For, by no means is that Being compelled or forbidden by a law of space or time to exist, or not to exist, at any place or time -- the Being which, in no wise, includes its own existence in space or time. For, when the supreme Being is said to exist in space or time, although the form of expression regarding it, and regarding local and temporal natures, is the same, because of the usage of language, yet the sense is different, because of the unlikeness of the objects of discussion. For in the latter case the same expression has two meanings, namely: (1) that these objects are present in those places and times in which they are said to be, and (2) that they are contained by these places and times themselves.

But in the case of the supreme Being, the first sense only is intended, namely, that it is present; not that it is also contained. If the usage of language permitted, it would, therefore, seem to be more fittingly said, that it exists *with* place or time, than that it exists *in* place or time. For the statement that a thing exists *in* another implies that it is *contained*, more than does the statement that it exists with another.

In no place or time, then, is this Being properly said to exist, since it is contained by no other at all. And yet it may be said, after a manner of its own, to be in every place or time, since whatever else exists is sustained by its presence, lest it lapse into nothingness. It exists in every place and time, because it is absent from none; and it exists in none, because it has no place or time, and has not taken to itself distinctions of place or time, neither here nor there, nor anywhere, nor then, nor now, nor at any time; nor does it exist in terms of this fleeting present, in which we live, nor has it existed, nor will it exist, in terms of past or future, since these are restricted to things finite and mutable, which it is not.

And yet, these properties of time and place can, in some sort, be ascribed to it, since it is just as truly present in all finite and mutable beings as if it were circumscribed by the same places, and suffered change by the same times.

We have sufficient evidence, then, to dispel the contradiction that threatened us; as to how the highest Being of all exists, everywhere and always, and nowhere and never, that is, in every place and time, and in no place or time, according to the consistent truth of different senses of the terms employed.

CHAPTER XXIII.

How it is better conceived to exist everywhere than in every place

BUT, since it is plain that this supreme Nature is not more truly in all places than in all existing things, not as if it were contained by them, but as containing all, by permeating all, why should it not be said to be everywhere, in this sense, that it may be understood rather to be in all existing things, than merely in all places, since this sense is supported by the truth of the fact, and is not forbidden by the proper signification of the word of place?

For we often quite properly apply terms of place to objects which are not places; as, when I say that the understanding is *there* in the soul, *where* rationality is. For, though *there* and *where* are adverbs of place, yet, by no local limitation, does the mind contain anything, nor is either rationality or understanding contained.

Hence, as regards the truth of the matter, the supreme Nature is more appropriately said to be everywhere, in this sense, that it is in all existing things, than in this sense, namely that it is merely in all places. And since, as the reasons set forth above show, it cannot exist otherwise, it must so be in all existing things, that it is one and the same, perfect whole in every individual thing simultaneously.

CHAPTER XXIV.

How it is better understood to exist always *than at* every time.

IT is also evident that this supreme Substance is without beginning and without end; that it has neither past, nor future, nor the temporal, that is, transient present in which we live; since its age, or eternity, which is nothing else than itself, is immutable and without parts. Is not, therefore, the term which seems to mean *all time* more properly understood, when applied to this Substance, to signify eternity, which is never unlike itself, rather than a changing succession of times, which is ever in some sort unlike itself?

Hence, if this Being is said to exist always; since, for it, it is the same to exist and to live, no better sense can be attached to this statement, than that it exists or lives eternally, that is, it possesses interminable life, as a perfect whole at once. For its eternity apparently is an interminable life, existing at once as a perfect whole.

For, since it has already been shown that this Substance is nothing else than its own life and its own eternity, is in no wise terminable, and does not exist, except as at once and perfectly whole, what else is true eternity, which is consistent with the nature of that Substance alone, than an interminable life, existing as at once and perfectly whole?

For this truth is, at any rate, clearly perceived from the single fact that true eternity belongs only to that substance which alone, as we have proved, was not created, but is the creator, since true eternity is conceived to be free from the limitations of beginning and end; and this is proved to be consistent with the nature of no created being, from the very fact that all such have been created from nothing.

CHAPTER XXV.

It cannot suffer change by any accidents [Accidents, as Anselm uses the term, are facts external to the essence of a being, which may yet be conceived to produce changes in a mutable being.]

BUT does not this Being, which has been shown to exist as in every way substantially identical with itself, sometimes exist as different from itself, at any rate accidentally? But how is it supremely immutable, if it can, I will not say, *be*, but, be conceived of, as variable by virtue of accidents? And, on the ocher hand, does it not partake of accident, since even this very fact that it is greater than all other natures and that it is unlike them seems to be an accident in its case (*illi accidere*)? But what is the inconsistency between susceptibility to certain facts, called *accidents*, and natural immutability, if from the undergoing of these accidents the substance undergoes no change?

For, of all the facts, called accidents, some are understood not to be present or absent without some variation in the subject of the accident -- all colors, for instance -- while others are known not to effect any change in a thing either by occurring or not occurring -- certain relations, for instance. For it is certain that I am neither older nor younger than a man who is not yet born, nor equal to him, nor like him. But I shall be able to sustain and to lose all these relations toward him, as soon as he shall have been born, according as he shall grow, or undergo change through divers qualities.

It is made clear, then, that of all those facts, called accidents, a part bring some degree of mutability in their train, while a part do not impair at all the immutability of that in whose case they occur. Hence, although the supreme Nature in its simplicity has never undergone such accidents as cause mutation, yet it does not disdain occasional expression in terms of those accidents which are in no wise inconsistent with supreme immutability; and yet there is no accident respecting its essence, whence it would be conceived of, as itself variable.

Whence this conclusion, also, may be reached, that it is susceptible of no accident; since, just as those accidents, which effect some change by their occurrence or non-occurrence, are by virtue of this very effect of theirs regarded as being true *accidents*, so those facts, which lack a like effect, are found to be improperly called accidents. Therefore, this Essence is always, in every way, substantially identical with itself; and it is never in any way different from itself, even accidentally. But, however it may be as to the proper signification of the term *accident*, this is undoubtedly true, that of the supremely immutable Nature no statement can be made, whence it shall be conceived of as mutable.

CHAPTER XXVI.

How this Being is said to be substance: it transcends all substance and is individually whatever it is.

BUT, if what we have ascertained concerning the simplicity of this Nature is established, how is it substance? For, though every substance is susceptible of admixture of difference, or, at any rate, susceptible of mutation by accidents, the immutable purity of this Being is inaccessible to admixture or mutation, in any form.

How, then, shall it be maintained that it is a substance of any kind, except as it is called *substance* for *being*, and so transcends, as it is above, every substance? For, as great as is the difference between that Being, which is through itself whatever it is, and which creates every other being from nothing, and a being, which is made whatever it is through another, from nothing; so much does the supreme Substance differ from these beings, which are not what it is. And, since it alone, of all natures, derives from itself, without the help of another nature, whatever existence it has, is it not whatever it is individually and apart from association with its creatures?

Hence, if it ever shares any name with other beings, doubtless a very different signification of that name is to be understood in its case.

CHAPTER XXVII.

It is not included among substances as commonly treated, yet it is a substance and an indivisible spirit.

IT is, therefore, evident that in any ordinary treatment of substance, this Substance cannot be included, from sharing in whose essence every nature is excluded. Indeed, since every substance is treated either as universal, i. e., as essentially common to more than one substance, as being a man is common to individual men; or as individual, having a universal essence in common with others, as individual men have in common with individual men the fact that they are men; does any one conceive that, in the treatment of other substances, that supreme Nature is included, which neither divides itself into more substances than one, nor unites with any other, by virtue of a common essence?

Yet, seeing that it not only most certainly exists, but exists in the highest degree of all things; and since the essence of anything is usually called its substance, doubtless if any worthy name can be given it, there is no objection to our calling it *substance*.

And since no worthier essence than spirit and body is known, and of these, spirit is more worthy than body, it must certainly be maintained that this Being is spirit and not body. But, seeing that one spirit has not any parts, and there cannot be more spirits than one of this kind, it must, by all means, be an indivisible spirit. For since, as is shown above, it is neither compounded of parts, nor can be conceived of as mutable, through any differences or accidents, it is impossible that it is divisible by any form of division.

CHAPTER XXVIII.

This Spirit exists simply, and created beings are not comparable with him.

IT seems to follow, then, from the preceding considerations, that the Spirit which exists in so wonderfully singular and so singularly wonderful a way of its own is in some sort unique; while other beings which seem to be comparable with it are not so.

For, by diligent attention it will be seen that that Spirit alone exists simply, and perfectly, and absolutely; while all other beings are almost non-existent, and hardly exist at all. For, seeing that of this Spirit, because of its immutable eternity, it can in no wise be said, in terms of any alteration, that it *was* or *will be*, but simply that it *is*; it is not now, by mutation, anything which it either was not at any time, or will not be in the future. Nor does it fail to be now what it was, or will be, at any time; but, whatever it is, it is, once for all, and simultaneously, and interminably. Seeing, I say, that its existence is of this character, it is rightly said itself to exist simply, and absolutely, and perfectly.

But since, on the other hand, all other beings, in accordance with some cause, have at some time been, or will be, by mutation, what they are not now; or, are what they were not, or will not be, at some time; and, since this former existence of theirs is no longer a fact; and that future existence is not yet a fact; and their existence in a transient, and most brief, and scarcely existing, present is hardly a fact -- since, then, they exist in such mutability, it is not unreasonably denied that they exist simply, and perfectly, and absolutely; and it is asserted that they are almost nonexistent, that they scarcely exist at all.

Again, since all beings, which are other than this Spirit himself, have come from non-existence to existence, not through themselves, but through another; and, since they return from existence to non-existence, so far as their own power is concerned, unless they are sustained through another being, is it consistent with their nature to exist simply, or perfectly, or absolutely, and not rather to be almost non-existent.

And since the existence of this ineffable Spirit alone can in no way be conceived to have taken inception from non-existence, or to be capable of sustaining any deficiency rising from what is in nonexistence; and since, whatever he is himself, he is not through another than himself, that is, than what he is himself, ought not his existence alone to be conceived of as simple, and perfect, and absolute?

But what is thus simply, and on every ground, solely perfect, simple, and absolute, this may very certainly be justly said to be in some sort unique. And, on the other hand, whatever is known to exist through a higher cause, and neither simply, nor perfectly, nor absolutely, but scarcely to exist, or to be almost non-existent -- this assuredly may be rightly said to be in some sort non-existent.

According to this course of reasoning, then, the creative Spirit alone exists, and all creatures are nonexistent; yet, they are not wholly non-existent, because, through that Spirit which alone exists absolutely, they have been made something from nothing.

CHAPTER XXIX.

His expression is identical with himself, and consubstantial with him, since there are not two spirits, but one.

BUT now, having considered these questions regarding the properties of the supreme Nature, which have occurred to me in following the guidance of reason to the present point, I think it reasonable to examine this Spirit's expression (*locutio*), through which all things were created.

For, though all that has been ascertained regarding this expression above has the inflexible strength of reason, I am especially compelled to a more careful discussion of this expression by the fact that it is proved to be identical with the supreme Spirit himself. For, if this Spirit created nothing except through himself, and whatever was created by him was created through that expression, how shall that expression be anything else than what the Spirit himself is?

Furthermore, the facts already discovered declare irrefutably that nothing at all ever could, or can, exist, except the creative Spirit and its creatures. But it is impossible that the expression of this Spirit is included among created beings; for every created being was created through that expression; but that expression could not be created through itself. For nothing can be created through itself, since every creature exists later than that through which it is created, and nothing exists later than itself.

The alternative remaining is, then, that this expression of the supreme Spirit, since it cannot be a creature, is no other than the supreme Spirit. Therefore, this expression itself can be conceived of as nothing else than the intelligence (*intelligentia*) of this Spirit, by which he conceives of (*intelligit*) all things. For, to him, what is expressing anything, according to this kind of expression, but conceiving of it? For he does not, like man, ever fail to express what he conceives.

If, then, the supremely simple Nature is nothing else than what its intelligence is, just as it is identical with its wisdom, necessarily, in the same way, it is nothing else than what its expression is. But, since it is already manifest that the supreme Spirit is one only, and altogether indivisible, this his expression must be so consubstantial with him, that they are not two spirits, but one.

CHAPTER XXX.

This expression does not consist of more words than one, but is one Word.

WHY, then, should I have any further doubt regarding that question which I dismissed above as doubtful, namely, whether this expression consists of more words than one, or of one? For, if it is so consubstantial with the supreme Nature that they are not two spirits, but one; assuredly, just as the latter is supremely simple, so is the former. It therefore does not consist of more words than one, but is one Word, through which all things were created.

CHAPTER XXXI.

This Word itself is not the likeness of created beings, but the reality of their being, while created beings are a kind of likeness of reality. --What natures are greater and more excellent than others.

BUT here, it seems to me, there arises a question that is not easy to answer, and yet must not be left in any ambiguity. For all words of that sort by which we express any objects in our mind, that is, conceive of them, are likenesses and images of the objects to which they correspond; and every likeness or image is more or less true, according as it more or less closely imitates the object of which it is the likeness.

What, then, is to be our position regarding the Word by which all things are expressed, and through which all were created? Will it be, or will it not be, the likeness of the things that have been created through itself? For, if it is itself the true likeness of mutable things, it is not consubstantial with supreme immutability; which is false. But, if it is not altogether true, and is merely a sort of likeness of mutable things, then the Word of supreme Truth is not altogether true; which is absurd. But if it has no likeness to mutable things, how were they created after its example?

But perhaps nothing of this ambiguity will remain if -- as the reality of a man is said to be the living man, but the likeness or image of a man in his picture -- so the reality of being is conceived of as in the Word, whose essence exists so supremely that in a certain sense it alone exists; while in these things which, in comparison with that Essence, are in some sort non-existent, and, yet were made something through, and according to, that Word, a kind of imitation of that supreme Essence is found.

For, in this way the Word of supreme Truth, which is also itself supreme Truth, will experience neither gain nor loss, according as it is more or less like its creatures. But the necessary inference will rather be, that every created being exists in so much the greater degree, or is so much the more excellent, the more like it is to what exists supremely, and is supremely great.

For on this account, perhaps, -- nay, not perhaps, but certainly, -- does every mind judge natures in any way alive to excel those that are not alive, the sentient to excel the non-sentient, the rational the irrational. For, since the supreme Nature, after a certain unique manner of its own, not only exists, but lives, and is sentient and rational, it is clear that, of all existing beings, that which is in some way alive is more like this supreme Nature, than that which is not alive at all; and what, in any way, even by a corporeal sense, cognises anything, is more like this Nature than what is not sentient at all; and what is rational, more than what is incapable of reasoning.

But it is clear, for a like reason, that certain natures exist in a greater or less degree than others. For, just as that is more excellent by nature which, through its natural essence, is nearer to the most excellent Being, so certainly that nature exists in a greater degree, whose essence is more like the supreme Essence. And I think that this can easily be ascertained as follows. If we should conceive any substance that is alive, and sentient, and rational, to be deprived of its reason, then of its sentience, then of its life, and finally of the bare existence that remains, who would fail to understand that the substance that is thus destroyed, little by little, is gradually brought to smaller and smaller degrees of existence, and at last to non-existence? But the attributes which, taken each by itself, reduce an essence to less and less degrees of existence, if assumed in order, lead it to greater and greater degrees.

It is evident, then, that a living substance exists in a greater degree than one that is not living, a sentient than a non-sentient, and a rational than a nonrational. So, there is no doubt that every substance exists in a greater degree, and is more excellent, according as it is more like that substance which exists supremely and is supremely excellent.

It is sufficiently clear, then, that in the Word, through which all things were created, is not their likeness, but their true and simple essence; while, in the things created, there is not a simple and absolute essence, but an imperfect imitation of that true Essence. Hence, it necessarily follows, that this Word is not more nor less true, according to its likeness to the things created, but every created nature has a higher essence and dignity, the more it is seen to approach that Word.

CHAPTER XXXII.

The supreme Spirit expresses himself by a coeternal Word.

BUT since this is true, how can what is simple Truth be the Word corresponding to those objects, of which it is not the likeness? Since every word by which an object is thus mentally expressed is the likeness of that object, if this is not the word corresponding to the objects that have been created through it, how shall we be sure that it is the Word? For every word is a word corresponding to some object. Therefore, if there were no creature, there would be no word.

Are we to conclude, then, that if there were no creature, that Word would not exist at all, which is the supreme self-sufficient Essence? Or, would the supreme Being itself, perhaps, which is the Word still be the eternal Being, but not the Word, if nothing were ever created through that Being? For, to what has not been, and is not, and will not be, then can be no word corresponding.

But, according to this reasoning, if there were never any being but the supreme Spirit, there would be no word at all in him. If there were no word in him, he would express nothing to himself; if he expressed nothing to himself, since, for him, expressing anything is the same with understanding or conceiving of it (*intelligere*), he would not understand or conceive of anything; if he understood or conceived of nothing, then the supreme Wisdom, which is nothing else than this Spirit, would understand or conceive of nothing; which is most absurd.

What is to be inferred? For, if it conceived of nothing, how would it be the supreme Wisdom? Or, if there were in no wise anything but it, of what would it conceive? Would it not conceive of itself? But how can it be even imagined that the supreme Wisdom, at any time does not conceive of itself; since a rational mind can remember not only itself, but that supreme Wisdom, and conceive of that Wisdom and of itself? For, if the human mind could have no memory or concept of that Wisdom or of itself, it would not distinguish itself at all from irrational creatures, and that Wisdom from the whole created world, in silent meditation by itself, as my mind does now.

Hence, that Spirit, supreme as he is eternal, is thus eternally mindful of himself, and conceives of himself after the likeness of a rational mind; nay, not after the likeness of anything; but in the first place that Spirit, and the rational mind after its likeness. But, if he conceives of himself eternally, he expresses himself eternally. If he expresses himself eternally, his Word is eternally with him. Whether, therefore, it be thought of in connection with no other existing being, or with other existing beings, the Word of that Spirit must be coeternal with him.

CHAPTER XXXIII.

He utters himself and what he creates by a single consubstantial Word.

BUT here, in my inquiry concerning the Word, by which the Creator expresses all that he creates, is suggested the word by which he, who creates all, expresses himself. Does he express himself, then, by one word, and what be creates by another; or does he rather express whatever he creates by the same word whereby he expresses himself?

For this Word also, by which he expresses himself, must be identical with himself, as is evidently true of the Word by which he expresses his creatures. For since, even if nothing but that supreme Spirit ever existed, urgent reason would still require the existence of that word by which he expresses himself, what is more true than that his Word is nothing else than what he himself is? Therefore, if he expresses himself and what he creates, by a Word consubstantial with himself, it is manifest that of the Word by which he expresses himself, and of the Word by which he expresses the created world, the substance is one.

How, then, if the substance is one, are there two words? But, perhaps, identity of substance does not compel us to admit a single Word. For the Creator himself, who speaks in these words, has the same substance with them, and yet is not the Word. But, undoubtedly the word by which the supreme Wisdom expresses itself may most fitly be called its Word on the former ground, namely, that it contains the perfect likeness of that Wisdom.

For, on no ground can it be denied that when a rational mind conceives of itself in meditation the image of itself arises in its thought, or rather the thought of the mind is itself its image, after its likeness, as if formed from its impression. For, whatever object the mind, either through representation of the body or through reason, desires to conceive of truly, it at least attempts to express its likeness, so far as it is able, in the mental concept itself. And the more truly it succeeds in this, the more truly does it think of the object itself; and, indeed, this fact is observed more clearly when it thinks of something else which it is not, and especially when it thinks of a material body. For, when I think of a man I know, in his absence, the vision of my thought forms such an image as I have acquired in memory through my ocular vision and this image is the word corresponding to the man I express by thinking of him.

The rational mind, then, when it conceives of itself in thought, has with itself its image born of itself that is, its thought in its likeness, as if formed from its impression, although it cannot, except in thought alone, separate itself from its image, which image is its word.

Who, then, can deny that the supreme Wisdom, when it conceives of itself by expressing itself, begets a likeness of itself consubstantial with it, namely, its Word? And this Word, although of a subject so uniquely important nothing can be said with sufficient propriety, may still not inappropriately be called the image of that Wisdom, its representation, just as it is called his likeness.

But the Word by which the Creator expresses the created world is not at all, in the same way, a word corresponding to the created world, since it is not this world's likeness, but its elementary essence. It therefore follows, that he does not express the created world itself by a word corresponding to the created world. To what, then, does the word belong, whereby he expresses it, if he does not express it by a word, belonging to itself? For what he expresses, he expresses by a word, and a word must belong to something, that is, it is the likeness of something. But if he expresses nothing but himself or his created world he can express nothing, except by a word corresponding to himself or to something else.

So, if he expresses nothing by a word belonging to the created world, whatever he expresses, he expresses by the Word corresponding to himself. By one and the same Word, then, he expresses himself and whatever he has made.

CHAPTER XXXIV.

How he can express the created world by his Word.

BUT how can objects so different as the creative and the created being be expressed by one Word, especially since that Word itself is coeternal with him who expresses them, while the created world is not coeternal with him? Perhaps, because be himself is supreme Wisdom and supreme Reason, in which are all things that have been created; just as a work which is made after one of the arts, not only when it is made, but before it is made, and after it is destroyed, is always in respect of the art itself nothing else than what that art is.

Hence, when the supreme Spirit expresses himself, he expresses all created beings. For, both before they were created, and now that they have been created, and after they are decayed or changed in any way, they are ever in him not what they are in themselves, but what this Spirit himself is. For, in themselves they are mutable beings, created according to immutable reason; while in him is the true first being, and the first reality of existence, the more like unto which those beings are in any way, the more really and excellently do they exist. Thus, it may reasonably be declared that, when the supreme Spirit expresses himself, he also expresses whatever has been created by one and the same Word.

CHAPTER XXXV.

Whatever has been created is in his Word and knowledge, life and truth.

BUT, since it is established that his word is consubstantial with him, and perfectly like him, it necessarily follows that all things that exist in him exist also, and in the same way, in his Word. Whatever has been created, then, whether alive or not alive, or howsoever it exists in itself, is very life and truth in him.

But, since knowing is the same to the supreme Spirit as conceiving or expressing, he must know all things that he knows in the same way in which he expresses or conceives of them. Therefore, just as all things are in his Word life and truth, so are they in his knowledge.

CHAPTER XXXVI.

In how incomprehensible a way he expresses or knows the objects created by him.

HENCE, it may be most clearly comprehended that how this Spirit expresses, or how he knows the created world, cannot be comprehended by human knowledge. For none can doubt that created substances exist far differently in themselves than in our knowledge. For, in themselves they exist by virtue of their own being; while in our knowledge is not their being, but their likeness.

We conclude, then, that they exist more truly in themselves than in our knowledge, in the same degree in which they exist more truly anywhere by virtue of their own being, than by virtue of their likeness. Therefore, since this is also an established truth, that every created substance exists more truly in the Word, that is, in the intelligence of the Creator, than it does in itself, in the same degree in which the creative being exists more truly than the created; how can the human mind comprehend of what kind is that expression and that knowledge, which is so much higher and truer than created substances; if our knowledge is as far surpassed by those substances as their likeness is removed from their being?

CHAPTER XXXVII.

Whatever his relation to his creatures, this relation his Word also sustains: yet both do not simultaneously sustain this relation as more than one being.

BUT since it has already been clearly demonstrated that the supreme Spirit created all things through his Word, did not the Word itself also create all things? For, since it is consubstantial with him, it must be the supreme essence of that of which it is the Word. But there is no supreme Essence, except one, which is the only creator and the only beginning of all things which have been created. For this Essence, through no other than itself, alone created all things from nothing. Hence, whatever the supreme Spirit creates, the same his Word also creates, and in the same way.

Whatever relation, then, the supreme Spirit bears to what he creates, this relation his Word also bears, and in the same way. And yet, both do not bear it simultaneously, as more than one, since there are not more supreme creative essences than one. Therefore, just as he is the creator and the beginning of the world, so is his Word also; and yet there are not two, but one creator and one beginning.

CHAPTER XXXVIII.

It cannot be explained why they are two, although they must be so.

OUR careful attention is therefore demanded by a peculiarity which, though most unusual in other beings, seems to belong to the supreme Spirit and his Word. For, it is certain that in each of these separately and in both simultaneously, whatever they are so exists that it is separately perfected in both, and yet does not admit plurality in the two. For although, taken separately, he is perfectly supreme Truth and Creator, and his Word is supreme Truth and Creator; yet both at once are not two truths or two creators.

But although this is true, yet it is most remarkably clear that neither he, whose is the Word, can be his own Word, nor can the Word be he, whose Word it is, although in so far as regards either what they are substantially, or what relation they bear to the created world, they ever preserve an indivisible unity. But in respect of the fact that he does not derive existence from that Word, but that Word from him, they admit an ineffable plurality, ineffable, certainly, for although necessity requires that they be two, it can in no wise be explained why they are two.

For although they may perhaps be called two equals, or some other mutual relation may in like manner be attributed to them, yet if it were to be asked what it is in these very relative expressions with reference to which they are used, it cannot be expressed plurally, as one speaks of two equal lines, or two like men. For, neither are there two equal spirits nor two equal creators, nor is there any dual expression which indicates either their essence or their relation to the created world; and there is no dual expression which designates the peculiar relation of the one to the other, since there are neither two words nor two images.

For the Word, by virtue of the fact that it is a word or image, bears a relation to the other, because it is Word and image only as it is the Word and image of something; and so peculiar are these attributes to the one that they are by no means predicable of the other. For he, whose is the Word and image, is neither image nor Word. It is, therefore, evident that it cannot be explained why they are two, the supreme Spirit and the Word, although by certain properties of each they are required to be two. For it is the property of the one to derive existence from the other, and the property of that other that the first derives existence from him.

CHAPTER XXXIX.

This Word derives existence from the supreme Spirit by birth.

AND this truth, it seems, can be expressed in no more familiar terms than when it is said to be the property of the one, to be born of the other; and of the other, that the first is born of him. For it is now clearly proved, that the Word of the supreme Spirit does not derive existence from him, as do those beings which have been created by him; but as Creator from Creator, supreme Being from supreme Being. And, to dispose of this comparison with all brevity, it is one and the same being which derives existence from one and the same being, and on such terms, that it in no wise derives existence, except from that being.

Since it is evident, then, that the Word of the supreme Spirit so derives existence from him alone, that it is completely analogous to the offspring of a parent; and that it does not derive existence from him, as if it were created by him, doubtless no more fitting supposition can be entertained regarding its origin, than that it derives existence from the supreme Spirit by birth (*nascendo*).

For, innumerable objects are unhesitatingly said to be born of those things from which they derive existence, although they possess no such likeness to those things of which they are said to be born, as offspring to a parent. -- We say, for instance, that the hair is born of the head, or the fruit of the tree, although the hair does not resemble the head, nor the fruit the tree.

If, then, many objects of this sort are without absurdity said to be born, so much the more fittingly may the Word of the supreme Spirit be said to derive existence from him by birth, the more perfect the resemblance it bears to him, like a child's to its parent, through deriving existence from him.

CHAPTER XL.

He is most truly a parent, and that Word his offspring.

BUT if it is most properly said to be born, and is so like him of whom it is born, why should it be esteemed *like*, as a child is like his parent? why should it not rather be declared, that the Spirit is more truly a parent, and the Word his offspring, the more he alone is sufficient to effect this birth, and the more what is born expresses his likeness? For, among other beings which we know bear the relations of parent and child, none so begets as to be solely and without accessory, sufficient to the generation of offspring; and none is so begotten that without any admixture of unlikeness, it shows complete likeness to its parent.

If, then, the Word of the supreme Spirit so derives its complete existence from the being of that Spirit himself alone, and is so uniquely like him, that no child ever so completely derives existence from its parent, and none is so like its parent, certainly the relation of parent and offspring can be ascribed to no beings so consistently as to the supreme Spirit and his Word. Hence, it is his property to be most truly parent, and its to be most truly his offspring.

CHAPTER XLI.

He most truly begets, and it is most truly begotten.

BUT it will be impossible to establish this proposition, unless, in equal degree, he most truly begets, and it is most truly begotten. As the former supposition is evidently true, so the latter is necessarily most certain. Hence, it belongs to the supreme Spirit most truly to beget, and to his Word to be most truly begotten.

CHAPTER XLII.

It is the property of the one to be most truly progenitor and Father, and of the other to be the begotten and Son.

I should certainly be glad, and perhaps able, now to reach the conclusion, that he is most truly the Father, while this Word is most truly his Son. But I think that even this question should not be neglected: whether it is more fitting to call them Father and Son, than mother and daughter, since in them there is no distinction of sex.

For, if it is consistent with the nature of the one to be the Father, and of his offspring to be the Son, because both are Spirit (*Spiritus*, masculine); why is it not, with equal reason, consistent with the nature of the one to be the mother, and the other the daughter, since both are truth and wisdom (*veritas et sapientia*, feminine)?

Or, is it because in these natures that have a difference of sex, it belongs to the superior sex to be father or son, and to the inferior to be mother or daughter? And this is certainly a natural fact in most instances, but in some the contrary is true, as among certain kinds of birds, among which the female is always larger and stronger, while the male is smaller and weaker.

At any rate, it is more consistent to call the supreme Spirit father than mother, for this reason, that the first and principal cause of offspring is always in the father. For, if the maternal cause is ever in some way preceded by the paternal, it is exceedingly inconsistent that the name *mother* should be attached to that parent with which, for the generation of offspring, no other cause is associated, and which no other precedes. It is, therefore, most true that the supreme Spirit is Father of his offspring. But, if the son is always more like the father than is the daughter, while nothing is more like the supreme Father than his offspring; then it is most true that this offspring is not a daughter, but a Son.

Hence, just as it is the property of the one most truly to beget, and of the other to be begotten, so it is the property of the one to be most truly progenitor, and of the other to be most truly begotten. And as the one is most truly the parent, and the other his offspring, so the one is most truly Father, and the other most truly Son.

CHAPTER XLIII.

Consideration of the common attributes of both and the individual properties of each.

Now that so many and so important properties of each have been discovered, whereby a strange plurality, as ineffable as it is inevitable, is proved to exist in the supreme unity, I think it most interesting to reflect, again and again, upon so unfathomable a mystery.

For observe: although it is so impossible that he who begets, and he who is begotten, are the same, and that parent and offspring are the same --so impossible that necessarily one must be the progenitor and the other the begotten, and one the Father, the other the Son; yet, here it is so necessary that he who begets and he who is begotten shall be the same, and also that parent and offspring shall be the same, that the progenitor cannot be any other than what the begotten is, nor the Father any other than the Son.

And although the one is one, and the other another, so that it is altogether evident that they are two; yet that which the one and the other are is in such a way one and the same, that it is a most obscure mystery why they are two. For, in such a way is one the Father and the other the Son, that when I speak of both I perceive that I have spoken of two; and yet so identical is that which both Father and Son are, that I do not understand why they are two of whom I have spoken.

For, although the Father separately is the perfectly supreme Spirit, and the Son separately is the perfectly supreme Spirit, yet, so are the Spirit-Father and the Spirit-Son one and the same being, that the Father and the Son are not two spirits, but one Spirit. For, just as to separate properties of separate beings, plurality is not attributed, since they are not properties of two things, so, what is common to both preserves an indivisible unity, although it belongs, as a whole, to them taken separately.

For, as there are not two fathers or two sons, but one Father and one Son, since separate properties belong to separate beings, so there are not two spirits, but one Spirit; although it belongs both to the Father, taken separately, and to the Son, taken separately, to be the perfect Spirit. For so opposite are their relations, that the one never assumes the property of the other; so harmonious are they in nature, that the one ever contains the essence of the other. For they are so diverse by virtue of the fact that the one is the Father and the other the Son, that the Father is never called the Son, nor the Son the Father; and they are so identical, by virtue of their substance, that the essence of the Son is ever in the Father, and the essence of the Father in the Son.

CHAPTER XLIV.

How one is the essence of the other.

HENCE, even if one is called the essence of the other, there is no departure from truth; but the supreme simplicity and unity of their common nature is thus honored. For, not as one conceives of a man's wisdom, through which man is wise, though he cannot be wise through himself, can we thus understand the statement that the Father is essence of the Son, and the Son the essence of the Father. We cannot understand that the Son is existent through the Father, and the Father through the Son, as if the one could not be existent except through the other, just as a man cannot be wise except through wisdom.

For, as the supreme Wisdom is ever wise through itself, so the supreme Essence ever exists through itself. But, the perfectly supreme Essence is the Father, and the perfectly supreme Essence is the Son. Hence, the perfect Father and the perfect Son exist, each through himself, just as each is wise through himself.

For the Son is not the less perfect essence or wisdom because he is an essence born of the essence of the Father, and a wisdom born of the wisdom of the Father; but he would be a less perfect essence or wisdom if he did not exist through himself, and were not wise through himself.

For, there is no inconsistency between the subsistence of the Son through himself, and his deriving existence from his Father. For, as the Father has essence, and wisdom, and life in himself; so that not through another's, but through his own, essence he exists; through his own wisdom he is wise; through his own life he lives; so, by generation, he grants to his Son the possession of essence, and wisdom, and life in himself, so that not through an extraneous essence, wisdom, and life, but through his own, he subsists, is wise, and lives; otherwise, the existence of Father and Son will not be the same, nor will the Son be equal to the Father. But it has already been clearly proved how false this supposition is.

Hence, there is no inconsistency between the subsistence of the Son through himself, and his deriving existence from the Father, since he must have from the Father this very power of subsisting through himself. For, if a wise man should teach me his wisdom, which I formerly lacked, he might without impropriety be said to teach me by this very wisdom of his. But, although my wisdom would derive its existence and the fact of its being from his wisdom, yet when my wisdom once existed, it would be no other essence than its own, nor would it be wise except through itself.

Much more, then, the eternal Father's eternal Son, who so derives existence from the Father that they are not two essences, subsists, is wise, and lives through himself. Hence, it is inconceivable that the Father should be the essence of the Son, or the Son the essence of the Father, on the ground that the one could not subsist through itself, but must subsist through the other. But in order to indicate how they share in an essence supremely simple and supremely one, it may consistently be said, and conceived, that the one is so identical with the other that the one possesses the essence of the other.

On these grounds, then, since there is obviously no difference between possessing an essence and being an essence, just as the one possesses the essence of the other, so the one is the essence of the other, that is, the one has the same existence with the other.

CHAPTER XLV.

The Son may more appropriately be called the essence of the Father, than the Father the essence of the Son: and in like manner the Son is the virtue, wisdom, etc., of the Father.

AND although, for reasons we have noted, this is true, it is much more proper to call the Son the essence of the Father than the Father the essence of the Son. For, since the Father has his being from none other than himself, it is not wholly appropriate to say that he has the being of another than himself; while, since the Son has his being from the Father, and has the same essence with his Father, he may most appropriately be said to have the essence of his Father.

Hence, seeing that neither has an essence, except by *being* an essence; as the Son is more appropriately conceived to have the essence of the Father than the Father to have the essence of the Son, so the Son may more fitly be called the essence of the Father than the Father the essence of the son. For this single explanation proves, with sufficiently emphatic brevity, that the Son not only has the same essence with the Father, but has this very essence from the Father; so that, to assert that the Son is the essence of the Father is the same as to assert that the Son is not a different essence from the essence of the Father nay, from the Father essence.

In like manner, therefore, the Son is the virtue of the Father, and his wisdom, and justice, and whatever is consistently attributed to the essence of the supreme Spirit.

CHAPTER XLVI.

How some of these truths which are thus expounded may also be conceived of in another way.

YET, some of these truths, which may be thus expounded and conceived of, are apparently capable of another interpretation as well, not inconsistent with this same assertion. For it is proved that the Son is the true Word, that is, the perfect intelligence, conceiving of the whole substance of the Father, or perfect cognition of that substance, and knowledge of it, and wisdom regarding it; that is, it understands, and conceives of, the very essence of the Father, and cognises it, and knows it, and is wise (*sapit*) regarding it.

If, then, in this sense, the Son is called the intelligence of the Father, and wisdom concerning him, and knowledge and cognition of him, and acquaintance with him; since the Son understands and conceives of the Father, is wise concerning him, knows and is acquainted with him, there is no departure from truth.

Most properly, too, may the Son be called the truth of the Father, not only in the sense that the truth of the Son is the same with that of the Father, as we have already seen; but in this sense, also, that in him no imperfect imitation shall be conceived of, but the complete truth of the substance of the Father since he is no other than what the Father is.

CHAPTER XLVII.

The Son is the intelligence of intelligence and the Truth of truth

BUT if the very substance of the Father is intelligence, and knowledge, and wisdom, and truth, it is consequently inferred that as the Son is the intelligence, and knowledge, and wisdom, and truth, of the paternal substance, so he is the intelligence of intelligence, the knowledge of knowledge, the wisdom of wisdom, and the truth of truth.

CHAPTER XLVIII.

How the Son is the intelligence or wisdom of memory or the memory of the Father and of memory.

BUT what is to be our notion of memory? Is the Son to be regarded as the intelligence conceiving of memory, or as the memory of the Father, or as the memory of memory? Indeed, since it cannot be denied that the supreme Wisdom remembers itself, nothing can be more consistent than to regard the Father as memory, just as the Son is the Word; because the Word is apparently born of memory, a fact that is more clearly seen in the case of the human mind.

For, since the human mind is not always thinking of itself, though it ever remembers itself, it is clear that, when it thinks of itself, the word corresponding to it is born of memory. Hence, it appears that, if it always thought of itself, its word would be always born of memory. For, to think of an object of which we have remembrance, this is to express it mentally; while the word corresponding to the object is the thought itself, formed after the likeness of that object from memory.

Hence, it may be clearly apprehended in the supreme Wisdom, which always thinks of itself, just as it remembers itself, that, of the eternal remembrance of it, its coeternal Word is born. Therefore, as the Word is properly conceived of as the child, the memory most appropriately takes the name of parent. If, then, the child which is born of the supreme Spirit alone is the child of his memory, there can be no more logical conclusion than that his memory is himself. For not in respect of the fact that he remembers himself does he exist in his own memory, like ideas that exist in the human memory, without being the memory itself; but he so remembers himself that he is his own memory.

It therefore follows that, just as the Son is the intelligence or wisdom of the Father, so he is that of the memory of the Father. But, regarding whatever the Son has wisdom or understanding, this he likewise remembers. The Son is, therefore, the memory of the Father, and the memory of memory, that is, the memory that remembers the Father, who is memory, just as he is the wisdom of the Father, and the wisdom of wisdom, that is, the wisdom wise regarding the wisdom of the Father; and the Son is indeed memory, born of memory, as he is wisdom, born of wisdom, while the Father is memory and wisdom born of none.

CHAPTER XLIX.

The supreme Spirit loves himself.

BUT, while I am here considering with interest the individual properties and the common attributes of Father and Son, I find none in them more pleasurable to contemplate than the feeling of mutual love. For how absurd it would be to deny that the supreme Spirit loves himself, just as he remembers himself, and conceives of himself! since even the rational human mind is convinced that it can love both itself and him, because it can remember itself and him, and can conceive of itself and of him; for idle and almost useless is the memory and conception of any object, unless, so far as reason requires, the object itself is loved or condemned. The supreme Spirit, then, loves himself, just as he remembers himself and conceives of himself.

CHAPTER L.

The same love proceeds equally from Father and Son.

IT is, at any rate, clear to the rational man that he does not remember himself or conceive of himself because he loves himself, but he loves himself because he remembers himself and conceives of himself; and that he could not love himself if he did not remember and conceive of himself. For no object is loved without remembrance or conception of it; while many things are retained in memory and conceived of that are not loved.

It is evident, then, that the love of the supreme Spirit proceeds from the fact that he remember himself and conceives of himself (*se intelligit*). But if, by the memory of the supreme Spirit, we understand the Father, and by his intelligence by which he conceives of anything, the Son, it is manifest that the love of the supreme Spirit proceeds equally from Father and Son.

CHAPTER LI.

Each loves himself and the other with equal love.

BUT if the supreme Spirit loves himself, no doubt the Father loves himself, the Son loves himself, and the one the other; since the Father separately is the supreme Spirit, and the Son separately is the supreme Spirit, and both at once one Spirit. And, since each equally remembers himself and the other, and conceives equally of himself and the other; and since what is loved, or loves in the Father, or in the Son, is altogether the same, necessarily each loves himself and the other with an equal love.

CHAPTER LII.

This love is as great as the supreme Spirit himself.

How great, then, is this love of the supreme Spirit, common as it is to Father and Son! But, if he loves himself as much as he remembers and conceives of himself; and, moreover, remembers and conceives of himself in as great a degree as that in which his essence exists, since otherwise it cannot exist; undoubtedly his love is as great as he himself is.

CHAPTER LIII.

This love is identical with the supreme Spirit, and yet it is itself with the Father and the Son one spirit.

BUT, what can be equal to the supreme Spirit, except the supreme Spirit? That love is, then, the supreme Spirit. Hence, if no creature, that is, if nothing other than the supreme Spirit, the Father and the Son, ever existed; nevertheless, Father and Son would love themselves and one another.

It therefore follows that this love is nothing else than what the Father and the Son are, which is the supreme Being. But, since there cannot be more than one supreme Being, what inference can be more necessary than that Father and Son and the love of both are one supreme Being? Therefore, this love is supreme Wisdom, supreme Truth, the supreme Good, and whatsoever can be attributed to the substance the supreme Spirit.

CHAPTER LIV.

It proceeds as a whole from the Father, and as a whole from the Son, and yet does not exist except as one love.

IT should be carefully considered whether there are two loves, one proceeding from the Father, the other from the Son; or one, not proceeding as a whole from one, but in part from the Father, in part from the Son; or neither more than one, nor one proceeding in part from each separately, but one proceeding as a whole from each separately, and likewise as a whole from the two at once.

But the solution of such a question can, without doubt, be apprehended from the fact that this love proceeds not from that in which Father and Son are more than one, but from that in which they are one. For, not from their relations, which are more than one, but from their essence itself, which does not admit of plurality, do Father and Son equally produce so great a good.

Therefore, as the Father separately is the supreme Spirit, and the Son separately is the supreme Spirit, and Father and Son at once are not two, but one Spirit; so from the Father separately the love of the supreme Spirit emanates as a whole, and from the Son as a whole, and at once from Father and Son, not as two, but as one and the same whole.

CHAPTER LV.

This love is not their Son.

SINCE this love, then, has its being equally from Father and Son, and is so like both that it is in no wise unlike them, but is altogether identical with them; is it to be regarded as their Son or offspring? But, as the Word, so soon as it is examined, declares itself to be the offspring of him from whom it derives existence, by displaying a manifold likeness to its parent; so love plainly denies that it sustains such a relation, since, so long as it is conceived to proceed from Father and Son, it does not at once show to one who contemplates it so evident a likeness to him from whom it derives existence, although deliberate reasoning teaches us that it is altogether identical with Father and Son.

Therefore, if it is their offspring, either one of them is its father and the other its mother, or each is its father, or mother, -- suppositions which apparently contradict all truth. For, since it proceeds in precisely the same way from the Father as from the Son, regard for truth does not allow the relations of Father and Son to it to be described by different words; therefore, the one is not its father, the other its mother. But that there are two beings which, taken separately, bear each the perfect relation of father or mother, differing in no respect, to some one being --of this no existing nature allows proof by any example.

Hence, both, that is, Father and Son, are not father and mother of the love emanating from them. It therefore is apparently most inconsistent with truth that their identical love should be their son or offspring.

CHAPTER LVI.

Only the Father begets and is unbegotten; only the son is begotten; only love neither begotten nor unbegotten.

STILL, it is apparent that this love can neither be said, in accordance with the usage of common speech, to be unbegotten, nor can it so properly be said to be begotten, as the Word is said to be begotten. For we often say of a thing that it is begotten of that from which it derives existence, as when we say that light or heat is begotten of fire, or any effect of its cause.

On this ground, then, love, proceeding from supreme Spirit, cannot be declared to be wholly unbegotten, but it cannot so properly be said to be begotten as can the Word; since the Word is the most true offspring and most true Son, while it is manifest that love is by no means offspring or son.

He alone, therefore, may, or rather should, be called begetter and unbegotten, whose is the Word; since he alone is Father and parent, and in no wise derives existence from another; and the Word alone should be called begotten, which alone is Son and offspring. But only the love of both is neither begotten nor unbegotten, because it is neither son nor offspring, and yet does in some sort derive existence from another.

CHAPTER LVII.

This love is uncreated and creator, as are Father and Son; and yet it is with them not three, but one uncreated and creative being. And it may be called the Spirit of Father and Son.

BUT, since this love separately is the supreme Being, as are Father and Son, and yet at once Father and Son, and the love of both are not more than one, but one supreme Being, which alone was created by none, and created all things through no other than itself; since this is true, necessarily, as the Father separately, and the Son separately, are each uncreated and creator, so, too, love separately is uncreated and creator, and yet all three at once are not more than one, but one uncreated and creative being.

None, therefore, makes or begets or creates the Father, but the Father alone begets, but does not create, the Son; while Father and Son alike do not create or beget, but somehow, if such an expression may be used, *breathe* their love: for, although the supremely immutable Being does not breathe after our fashion, yet the truth that this Being sends forth this, its love, which proceeds from it, not by departing from it, but by deriving existence from it, can perhaps be no better expressed than by saying that this Being *breathes* its love.

But, if this expression is admissible, as the Word of the supreme Being is its Son, so its love may fittingly enough be called its breath (*Spiritus*). So that, though it is itself essentially spirit, as are Father and Son, they are not regarded as the spirits of anything, since neither is the Father born of any other nor the Son of the Father, as it were, by *breathing*; while that love is regarded as the Breath or Spirit of both since from both breathing in their transcendent way it mysteriously proceeds.

And this love, too, it seems, from the fact there is community of being between Father and Son, may, not unreasonably, take, as it were its own, some name which is common to Father and Son; if there is any exigency demanding that it should have a name proper to itself. And, indeed, if this love is actually designated by the name Spirit, as by its own name, since this name equally describes the Father and the Son: it will be useful to this effect also, that through this name it shall be signified that this love is identical with Father and Son, although it has its being from them.

CHAPTER LVIII.

As the Son is the essence or wisdom of the Father in the sense that he has the same essence or wisdom that the Father has: so likewise the Spirit is the essence and wisdom etc. of Father and Son.

ALSO, just as the Son is the substance and wisdom and virtue of the Father, in the sense that he has the same essence and wisdom and virtue with the Father; so it may be conceived that the Spirit of both is the essence or wisdom or virtue of Father and Son, since it has altogether the same essence, wisdom, and virtue with these.

CHAPTER LIX.

The Father and the Son and their Spirit exist equally the one in the other.

IT is a most interesting consideration that the Father, and the Son, and the Spirit of both, exist in one another with such equality that no one of them surpasses another. For, not only is each in such a way the perfectly supreme Being that, nevertheless, all three at once exist only as one supreme Being, but he same truth is no less capable of proof when each is taken separately.

For the Father exists as a whole in the Son, and in the Spirit common to them; and the Son in the Father, and in the Spirit; and the Spirit in the Father, and in the Son; for the memory of the supreme Being exists, as a whole, in its intelligence and in its love, and the intelligence in its memory and love, and the love in its memory and intelligence. For the supreme Spirit conceives of (*intelligit*) its memory as a whole, and loves it, and remembers its intelligence as a whole, and loves it as a whole, and remembers its love as a whole, and conceives of it as a whole.

But we mean by the memory, the Father; by the intelligence, the Son; by the love, the Spirit of both. In such equality, therefore, do Father and Son and Spirit embrace one another, and exist in one another, that none of them can be proved to surpass another or to exist without it.

CHAPTER LX.

To none of these is another necessary that he may remember, conceive, or love: since each taken by himself is memory and intelligence and love and all that is necessarily inherent in the supreme Being.

BUT, while this discussion engages our attention, I think that this truth, which occurs to me as I reflect, ought to be most carefully commended to memory. The Father must be so conceived of as memory, the Son as intelligence, and the Spirit as love, that it shall also be understood that the Father does not need the Son, or the Spirit common to them, nor the Son the Father, or the same Spirit, nor the Spirit the Father, or the Son: as if the Father were able, through his own power, only to remember, but to conceive only through the Son, and to love only through the Spirit of himself and his son; and the Son could only conceive or understand (*intelligere*) through himself, but remembered through the Father, and loved through his Spirit; and this Spirit were able through himself alone only to love, while the Father remembers for him, and the Son conceives or understands (*intelligit*) for him.

For, since among these three each one taken separately is so perfectly the supreme Being and the supreme Wisdom that through himself he remembers and conceives and loves, it must be that none of these three needs another, in order either to remember or to conceive or to love. For, each taken separately is essentially memory and intelligence and love, and all that is necessarily inherent in the supreme Being.

CHAPTER LXI.

Yet there are not three, but one Father and one Son and one Spirit.

AND here I see a question arises. For, if the Father is intelligence and love as well as memory, and the Son is memory and love as well as intelligence, and the Spirit is no less memory and intelligence than love; how is it that the Father is not a Son and a Spirit of some being? and why is not the Son the Father and the Spirit of some being? and why is not this Spirit the Father of some being, and the Son of some being? For it was understood, that the Father was memory, the Son intelligence, and the Spirit love.

But this question is easily answered, if we consider the truths already disclosed in our discussion. For the Father, even though he is intelligence and love, is not for that reason the Son or the Spirit of any being; since he is not intelligence, begotten of any, or love, proceeding from any, but whatever he is, he is only the *begetter*, and is he from whom the other proceeds.

The Son also, even though by his own power he remembers and loves, is not, for that reason, the Father or the Spirit of any; since he is not memory as begetter, or love as proceeding from another after the likeness of his Spirit, but whatever being he has he is only *begotten* and is he from whom the Spirit proceeds.

The Spirit, too, is not necessarily Father or Son, because his own memory and intelligence are sufficient to him; since he is not memory as begetter, or intelligence as begotten, but he alone, whatever he is, *proceeds* or *emanates*.

What, then, forbids the conclusion that in the supreme Being there is only one Father, one Son, one Spirit, and not three Fathers or Sons or Spirits?

CHAPTER LXII.

How it seems that of these three more sons than one are born.

BUT perhaps the following observation will prove inconsistent with this assertion. It should not be doubted that the Father and the Son and their Spirit each expresses himself and the other two, just as each conceives of, and understands, himself and the other two. But, if this is true, are there not in the supreme Being as many words as there are expressive beings, and as many words as there are beings who are expressed?

For, if more men than one give expression to some one object in thought, apparently there are as many words corresponding to that object as there are thinkers; since the word corresponding to it exists in the thoughts of each separately. Again, if one man thinks of more objects than one, there are as many words in the mind of the thinker as there are objects thought of.

But in the thought of a man, when he thinks of anything outside his own mind, the word corresponding to the object thought of is not born of the object itself, since that is absent from the view of thought, but of some likeness or image of the object which exists in the memory of the thinker, or which is perhaps called to mind through a corporeal sense from the present object itself.

But in the supreme Being, Father and Son and their Spirit are always so present to one another -- for each one, as we have already seen, exists in the others no less than in himself -- that, when they express one another, the one that is expressed seems to beget his own word, just as when he is expressed by himself. How is it, then, that the Son and the Spirit of the Son and of the Father beget nothing, if each begets his own word, when he is expressed by himself or by another? Apparently as many words as can be proved to be born of the supreme Substance, so many Sons, according to our former reasoning, must there be begotten of this substance, and so many spirits proceeding from it.

CHAPTER LXIII.

How among them there is only one Son of one Father, that is, one Word, and that from the Father alone.

ON these grounds, therefore, there apparently are in that Being, not only many fathers and sons and beings proceeding from it, but other necessary attributes as well; or else Father and Son and their Spirit, of whom it is already certain that they truly exist, are not three expressive beings, although each taken separately is expressive, nor are there more beings than one expressed, when each one expresses himself and the other two.

For, just as it is an inherent property of the supreme Wisdom to know and conceive, so it is assuredly natural to eternal and immutable knowledge and intelligence ever to regard as present what it knows and conceives of. For, to such a supreme Spirit expressing and beholding through conception, as it were, are the same, just as the expression of our human mind is nothing but the intuition of the thinker.

But reasons already considered have shown most convincingly that whatever is essentially inherent in the supreme Nature is perfectly consistent with the nature of the Father and the Son and their Spirit taken separately; and that, nevertheless, this, if attributed to the three at once, does not admit of plurality. Now, it is established that as knowledge and intelligence are attributes of his being, so his knowing and conceiving is nothing else than his expression, that is, his ever beholding as present what he knows and conceives of. Necessarily, therefore, just as the Father separately, and the Son separately, and their Spirit separately, is a knowing and conceiving being, and yet the three at once are not more knowing and conceiving beings than one, but one knowing and one conceiving being: so, each taken separately is expressive, and yet there are not three expressive beings at once, but one expressive being.

Hence, this fact may also be clearly recognised, that when these three are expressed, either by themselves or by another, there are not more beings than one expressed. For what is therein expressed except their being? If, then, that Being is one and only one, then what is expressed is one and only one; therefore, if it is in them one and only one which expresses, and one which is expressed --for it is one wisdom which expresses and one substance which is expressed --it follows that there are not more words than one, but one alone. Hence, although each one expresses himself and all express one another, nevertheless there cannot be in the supreme Being another Word than that already shown to be born of him whose is the Word, so that it may be called his true image and his Son.

And in this truth I find a strange and inexplicable factor. For observe: although it is manifest that each one, that is, Father and Son, and the Spirit of Father and Son equally expresses himself and both the others, and that there is one Word alone among them; yet it appears that this Word itself can in no wise be called the Word of all three, but only of one.

For it has been proved that it is the image and Son of him whose Word it is. And it is plain that it cannot properly be called either the image or son of itself, or of the Spirit proceeding from it. For, neither of itself nor of a being proceeding from it, is it born, nor does it in its existence imitate itself or a being proceeding from itself. For it does not imitate itself, or take on a like existence to itself, because imitation and likeness are impossible where only one being is concerned, but require plurality of beings; while it does not imitate the spirit, nor does it exist in his likeness, because it has not its existence from that Spirit, but the Spirit from it. It is to be concluded that this sole Word corresponds to him alone, from whom it has existence by generation, and after whose complete likeness it exists.

One Father, then, and not more than one Father; one Son, and not more than one Son; one Spirit proceeding from them, and not more than one such Spirit, exist in the supreme Being. And, although there are three, so that the Father is never the Son or the Spirit proceeding from them, nor the Son at any time the Father or the Spirit, nor the Spirit of Father and Son ever the Father or the Son; and each separately is so perfect that he is self-sufficient, needing neither of the others; yet what they are is in such a way one that just as it cannot be attributed to them taken separately as plural, so, neither can it be attributed to them as plural, when the three are taken at once. And though each one expresses himself and all express one another, yet there are not among them more words than one, but one; and this Word corresponds not to each separately, nor to all together, but to one alone.

CHAPTER LXIV.

Though this truth is inexplicable, it demands belief.

IT seems to me that the mystery of so sublime a subject transcends all the vision of the human intellect. And for that reason I think it best to refrain from the attempt to explain how this thing is. For it is my opinion that one who is investigating an incomprehensible object ought to be satisfied if this reasoning shall have brought him far enough to recognise that this object most certainly exists; nor ought assured belief to be the less readily given to these truths which are declared to be such by cogent proofs, and without the contradiction of any other reason, if, because of the incomprehensibility of their own natural sublimity, they do not admit of explanation.

But what is so incomprehensible, so ineffable, as that which is above all things? Hence, if these truths, which have thus far been debated in connection with the supreme Being, have been declared on cogent grounds, even though they cannot be so examined by the human intellect as to be capable of explanation in words, their assured certainty is not therefore shaken. For, if a consideration, such as that above, rationally comprehends that it is incomprehensible in what way supreme Wisdom knows its creatures, of which we necessarily know so many; who shall explain how it knows and expresses itself, of which nothing or scarcely anything can be known by man? Hence, if it is not by virtue of the self-expression of this Wisdom that the Father begets and the Son is begotten, *who shall tell his generation?*

CHAPTER LXV.

How real truth may be reached in the discussion of an ineffable subject.

BUT again, if such is the character of its ineffability, -- nay, since it is such, -- how shall whatever conclusion our discussion has reached regarding it in terms of Father, Son, and emanating Spirit be valid? For, if it has been explained on true grounds, how is it ineffable? Or, if it is ineffable, how can it be such as our discussion has shown? Or, could it be explained to a certain extent, and therefore nothing would disprove the truth of our argument; but since it could not be comprehended at all, for that reason it would be ineffable?

But how shall we meet the truth that has already been established in this very discussion, namely, that the supreme Being is so above and beyond every other nature that, whenever any statement is made concerning it in words which are also applicable to other natures, the sense of these words in this case is by no means that in which they are applied to other natures.

For what sense have I conceived of, in all these words that I have thought of, except the common and familiar sense? If, then, the familiar sense of words is alien to that Being, whatever I have inferred to be attributable to it is not its property. How, then, has any truth concerning the supreme Being been discovered, if what has been discovered is so alien to that Being? What is to be inferred?

Or, has there in some sort been some truth discovered regarding this incomprehensible object, and in some sort has nothing been proved regarding it? For often we speak of things which we do not express with precision as they are; but by another expression we indicate what we are unwilling or unable to express with precision, as when we speak in riddles. And often we see a thing, not precisely as it is in itself, but through a likeness or image, as when we look upon a face in a mirror. And in this way, we often express and yet do not express, see and yet do not see, one and the same object; we express and see it through another; we do not express it, and do not see it by virtue of its own proper nature.

On these grounds, then, it appears that there is nothing to disprove the truth of our discussion thus far concerning the supreme Nature, and yet this Nature itself remains not the less ineffable, if we believe that it has never been expressed according to the peculiar nature of its own being, but somehow described through another.

For whatever terms seem applicable to that Nature do not reveal it to me in its proper character, but rather intimate it through some likeness. For, when I think of the meanings of these terms, I more naturally conceive in my mind of what I see in created objects, than of what I conceive to transcend all human understanding. For it is something much less, nay, something far different, that their meaning suggests to my mind, than that the conception of which my mind itself attempts to achieve through this shadowy signification.

For, neither is the term *wisdom* sufficient to reveal to me that Being, through which all things were created from nothing and are preserved from nothingness; nor is the term *essence* capable of expressing to me that Being which, through its unique elevation, is far above all things, and through its peculiar natural character greatly transcends all things.

In this way, then, is that Nature ineffable, because it is incapable of description in words or by any other means; and, at the same time, an inference regarding it, which can be reached by the instruction of reason or in some other way, as it were in a riddle, is not therefore necessarily false.

CHAPTER LXVI.

Through the rational mind is the nearest approach to the supreme Being.

SINCE it is clear, then, that nothing can be ascertained concerning this Nature in terms of its own peculiar character, but only in terms of something else, it is certain that a nearer approach toward knowledge of it is made through that which approaches it more nearly through likeness. For the more like to it anything among created beings is proved to be, the more excellent must that created being be by nature. Hence, this being, through its greater likeness, assists the investigating mind in the approach to supreme Truth; and through its more excellent created essence, teaches the more correctly what opinion the mind itself ought to form regarding the Creator. So, undoubtedly, a greater knowledge of the creative Being is attained, the more nearly the creature through which the investigation is made approaches that Being. For that every being, in so far as it exists, is like the supreme Being, reasons already considered do not permit us to doubt.

It is evident, then, that as the rational mind alone, among all created beings, is capable of rising to the investigation of this Being, so it is not the less this same rational mind alone, through which the mind itself can most successfully achieve the discovery of this same Being. For it has already been acknowledged that this approaches it most nearly, through likeness of natural essence. What is more obvious, then, than that the more earnestly the rational mind devotes itself to learning its own nature, the more effectively does it rise to the knowledge of that Being; and the more carelessly it contemplates itself, the farther does it descend from the contemplation of that Being?

CHAPTER LXVII.

The mind itself is the mirror and image of that Being.

THEREFORE, the mind may most fitly be said to be its own mirror wherein it contemplates, so to speak, the image of what it cannot see face to face. For, if the mind itself alone among all created beings is capable of remembering and conceiving of and loving itself, I do not see why it should be denied that it is the true image of that being which, through its memory and intelligence and love, is united in an ineffable Trinity. Or, at any rate, it proves itself to be the more truly the image of that Being by its power of remembering, conceiving of, and loving, that Being. For, the greater and the more like that Being it is, the more truly it is recognised to be its image.

But, it is utterly inconceivable that any rational creature can have been naturally endowed with any power so excellent and so like the supreme Wisdom as this power of remembering, and conceiving of, and loving, the best and greatest of all beings. Hence, no faculty has been bestowed on any creature that is so truly the image of the Creator.

CHAPTER LXVIII.

The rational creature was created in order that it might love this Being.

IT seems to follow, then, that the rational creature ought to devote itself to nothing so earnestly as to the expression, through voluntary performance, of this image which is impressed on it through a natural potency. For, not only does it owe its very existence to its creator; but the fact that it is known to have no power so important as that of remembering, and conceiving of, and loving, the supreme good, proves that it ought to wish nothing else so especially.

For who can deny that whatever within the scope one's power is better, ought to prevail with the will? For, to the rational nature rationality is the same with the ability to distinguish the just from the not-just, the true from the not-true, the good from the not-good, the greater good from the lesser; but this power is altogether useless to it, and superfluous, unless what it distinguishes it loves or condemns, in accordance with the judgment of true discernment.

From this, then, it seems clear enough that every rational being exists for this purpose, that according as, on the grounds of discernment, it judges a thing to be more or less good, or not good, so it may love that thing in greater or less degree, or reject it.

It is, therefore, most obvious that the rational creature was created for this purpose, that it might love the supreme Being above all other goods, as this Being is itself the supreme good; nay, that it might love nothing except it, unless because of it; since that Being is good through itself, and nothing else is good except through it.

But the rational being cannot love this Being, unless it has devoted itself to remembering and conceiving of it. It is clear, then, that the rational creature ought to devote its whole ability and will to remembering, and conceiving of, and loving, the supreme good, for which end it recognises that it has its very existence.

CHAPTER LXIX.

The soul that ever loves this Essence lives at some time in true blessedness.

BUT there is no doubt that the human soul is a rational creature. Hence, it must have been created for this end, that it might love the supreme Being. It must, therefore, have been created either for this end, that it might love that Being eternally; or for this, that at some time it might either voluntarily, or by violence, lose this love.

But it is impious to suppose that the supreme Wisdom created it for this end, that at some time, either it should despise so great a good, or, though wishing to keep it, should lose it by some violence. We infer, then, that it was created for this end, that it might love the supreme Being eternally. But this it cannot do unless it lives forever. It was so created, then, that it lives forever, if it forever wills to do that for which it was created.

Hence, it is most incompatible with the nature of the supremely good, supremely wise, and omnipotent Creator, that what he has made to exist that it might love him, he should make not to exist, so long as it truly loves him; and that what he voluntarily gave to a non-loving being that it might ever love, he should take away, or permit to be taken away, from the loving being, so that necessarily it should not love; especially since it should by no means be doubted that he himself loves every nature that loves him. Hence, it is manifest that the human soul is never deprived of its life, if it forever devotes itself to loving the supreme life.

How, then, shall it live? For is long life so important a matter, if it is not secure from the invasion of troubles? For whoever, while he lives, is either through fear or through actual suffering subject to troubles, or is deceived by a false security, does he not live in misery? But, if any one lives in freedom from these troubles, he lives in blessedness. But it is most absurd to suppose that any nature that forever loves him, who is supremely good and omnipotent, forever lives in misery. So, it is plain, that the human soul is of such a character that, if it diligently observes that end for which it exists, it at some time lives in blessedness, truly secure from death itself and from every other trouble.

CHAPTER LXX.

This Being gives itself in return to the creature that loves it, that that creature may be eternally blessed.

THEREFORE it cannot be made to appear true that he who is most just and most powerful makes no return to the being that loves him perseveringly, to which although it neither existed nor loved him, he gave existence that it might be able to be a loving being. For, if he makes no return to the loving soul, the most just does not distinguish between the soul that loves, and the soul that despises what ought to be supremely loved, nor does he love the soul that loves him; or else it does not avail to be loved by him; all of which suppositions are inconsistent with his nature; hence he does make a return to every soul that perseveres in loving him.

But what is this return? For, if he gave to what was nothing, a rational being, that it might be a loving soul, what shall he give to the loving soul, if it does not cease to love? If what waits upon love is so great, how great is the recompense given to love? And if the sustainer of love is such as we declare, of what character is the profit? For, if the rational creature, which is useless to itself without this love, is with it preeminent among all creatures, assuredly nothing can be the reward of love except what is preeminent among all natures.

For this same good, which demands such love toward itself, also requires that it be desired by the loving soul. For, who can love justice, truth, blessedness, incorruptibility, in such a way as not to wish to enjoy them? What return, then, shall the supreme Goodness make to the being that loves and desires it, except itself? For, whatever else it grants, it does not give in return, since all such bestowals neither compensate the love, nor console the loving being, nor satisfy the soul that desires this supreme Being.

Or, if it wishes to be loved and desired, so as to make some other return than its love, it wishes to be loved and desired, not for its own sake, but for the sake of another; and does not wish to be loved itself, but wishes another to be loved; which it is impious to suppose.

So, it is most true that every rational soul, if, as it should, it earnestly devotes itself through love to longing for supreme blessedness, shall at some time receive that blessedness to enjoy, that what it now sees as *through a glass* and *in a riddle*, it may then see *face to face*. But it is most foolish to doubt whether it enjoys that blessedness eternally; since, in the enjoyment of that blessedness, it will be impossible to turn the soul aside by any fear, or to deceive it by false security; nor, having once experienced the need of that blessedness, will it be able not to love it; nor will that blessedness desert the soul that loves it; nor shall there be anything powerful enough to separate them against their will. Hence, the soul that has once begun to enjoy supreme Blessedness will be eternally blessed.

CHAPTER LXXI.

The soul that despises this being will be eternally miserable.

FROM this it may be inferred, as a certain consequence, that the soul which despises the love of the supreme good will incur eternal misery. It might be said that it would be justly punished for such contempt if it *lost* existence or life, since it does not employ itself to the end for which it was created. But reason in no wise admits such a belief, namely, that after such great guilt it is condemned to be what it was before all its guilt.

For, before it existed, it could neither be guilty nor feel a penalty. If, then, the soul despising that end for which it was created, dies so as to feel nothing, or so as to be nothing at all, its condition will be the same when in the greatest guilt and when without all guilt; and the supremely wise Justice will not distinguish between what is capable of no good and wills no evil, and what is capable of the greatest good and wills the greatest evil.

But it is plain enough that this is a contradiction. Therefore, nothing can be more logical, and nothing ought to be believed more confidently than that the soul of man is so constituted that, if it scorns loving the supreme Being, it suffers eternal misery; that just as the loving soul shall rejoice in an eternal reward, so the soul despising that Being shall suffer eternal punishment; and as the former shall feel an immutable sufficiency, so the latter shall feel an inconsolable need.

CHAPTER LXXII.

Every human soul is immortal. And it is either forever miserable, or at some time truly blessed.

BUT if the soul is mortal, of course the loving soul is not eternally blessed, nor the soul that scorns this Being eternally miserable. Whether, therefore, it loves or scorns that for the love of which it was created, it must be immortal. But if there are some rational souls which are to be judged as neither loving nor scorning, such as the souls of infants seem to be, what opinion shall be held regarding these? Are they mortal or immortal? But undoubtedly all human souls are of the same nature. Hence, since it is established that some are immortal, every human soul must be immortal. But since every living being is either never, or at some time, truly secure from all trouble; necessarily, also, every human soul is either ever miserable, or at some time truly blessed.

CHAPTER LXXIII.

No soul is unjustly deprived of the supreme good, and every effort must be directed toward that good.

BUT, which souls are unhesitatingly to be judged as so loving that for the love of which they were created, that they deserve to enjoy it at some time, and which as so scorning it, that they deserve ever to stand in need of it; or how and on what ground those which it seems impossible to call either loving or scorning are assigned to either eternal blessedness or misery, -- of all this I think it certainly most difficult or even impossible for any mortal to reach an understanding through discussion. But that no being is unjustly deprived by the supremely great and supremely good Creator of that good for which it was created, we ought most assuredly to believe. And toward this good every man ought to strive, by loving and desiring it with all his heart, and all his soul, and all his mind.

CHAPTER LXXIV.

The supreme Being is to be hoped for.

BUT the human soul will by no means be able to train itself in this purpose, if it despairs of being able to reach what it aims at. Hence, devotion to effort is not more profitable to it than hope of attainment is necessary.

CHAPTER LXXV.

We must believe in this Being, that is, by believing we must reach out for it.

BUT what does not believe cannot love or hope. It is, therefore, profitable to this human soul to believe the supreme Being and those things without which that Being cannot be loved, that, by believing, the soul may reach out for it. And this truth can be more briefly and fitly indicated, I think, if instead of saying, "strive for" the supreme Being, we say, "believe *in*" the supreme Being.

For, if one says that he believes *in* it, he apparently shows clearly enough both that, through the faith which he professes, he strives for the supreme Being, and that he believes those things which are proper to this aim. For it seems that either he who does not believe what is proper to striving for that Being, or he who does not strive for that Being, through what he believes, does not believe *in* it. And, perhaps, it is indifferent whether we say, "believe *in* it," or "direct belief *to* it," just as by believing to strive *for* it and *toward* it are the same, except that whoever shall have come to it by striving for (*tendendo in*) it, will not remain without, but within it. And this is indicated more distinctly and familiarly if we say, "striving *for*" (*in*) it, than if we say, "*toward*" (*ad*) it.

On this ground, therefore, I think it may more fitly be said that we should believe *in* it, than that we should direct belief *to* it.

CHAPTER LXXVI.

We should believe in Father and Son and in their Spirit equally, and in each separately, and in the three at once.

WE should believe, then, equally in the Father and in the Son and in their Spirit, and in each separately, and in the three at once, since the Father separately, and the Son separately, and their Spirit separately is the supreme Being, and at once Father and Son with their Spirit are one and the same supreme Being, in which alone every man ought to believe; because it is the sole end which in every thought and act he ought to strive for. Hence, it is manifest that as none is able to strive for that Being, except he believe in it; so to believe it avails none, except he strive for it.

CHAPTER LXXVII.

What is living, and what dead faith.

HENCE, with however great confidence so important a truth is believed, the faith will be useless and, as it were, dead, unless it is strong and living through love. For, that the faith which is accompanied by sufficient love is by no means idle, if an opportunity of operation offers, but rather exercises itself in an abundance of works, as it could not do without love, may be proved from this fact alone, that, since it loves the supreme Justice, it can scorn nothing that is just, it can approve nothing that is unjust. Therefore, seeing that the fact of its operation shows that life, without which it could not operate, is inherent in it; it is not absurd to say that operative faith is alive, because it has the life of love without which it could not operate; and that idle faith is not living, because it lacks that life of love, with which it would not be idle.

Hence, if not only he who has lost his sight is called blind, but also he who ought to have sight and has it not, why cannot, in like manner, *faith without love* be called *dead*; not because it has lost its life, that is, love; but because it has not the life which it ought always to have? As that faith, then, which operates through love is recognised as living, so that which is idle, through contempt, is proved to be dead. It may, therefore, be said with sufficient fitness that living faith believes *in* that *in* which we ought to believe; while dead faith merely believes that which ought to be believed.

CHAPTER LXXVIII.

The supreme Being may in some sort be called Three.

AND so it is evidently expedient for every man to believe in a certain ineffable trinal unity, and in one Trinity; one and a unity because of its one essence, but trinal and a trinity because of its three --what? For, although I can speak of a Trinity because of Father and Son and the Spirit of both, who are three; yet I cannot, in one word, show why they are three; as if I should call this Being a Trinity because of its three persons, just as I would call it a unity because of its one substance.

For three persons are not to be supposed, because all persons which are more than one so subsist separately from one another, that there must be as many substances as there are persons, a fact that is recognised in the case of more men than one, when there are as many persons as there are individual substances. Hence, in the supreme Being, just as there are not more substances than one, so there are not more persons than one.

So, if one wishes to express to any why they are three, he will say that they are Father and Son and the Spirit of both, unless perchance, compelled by the lack of a precisely appropriate term, he shall choose some one of those terms which cannot be applied in a plural sense to the supreme Being, in order to indicate what cannot be expressed in any fitting language; as if he should say, for instance, that this wonderful Trinity is one essence or nature, and three persons or substances.

For these two terms are more appropriately chosen to describe plurality in the supreme Being, because the word *person* is applied only to an individual, rational nature; and the word substance is ordinarily applied to individual beings, which especially subsist in plurality. For individual beings are especially exposed to, that is, are *subject* to, accidents, and for this reason they more properly receive the name *sub-stance*. Now, it is already manifest that the supreme Being, which is subject to no accidents, cannot properly be called a substance, except as the word *substance* is used in the same sense with the word *Essence*. Hence, on this ground, namely, of necessity, that supreme and one Trinity or trinal unity may justly be called one Essence and three Persons or three Substances.

CHAPTER LXXIX.

This Essence itself is God, who alone is lord and ruler of all.

IT appears, then -- nay, it is unhesitatingly declared that what is called God is not nothing; and that to this supreme Essence the name *God* is properly given. For every one who says that a God exists, whether one or more than one, conceives of him only as of some substance which be believes to be above every nature that is not God, and that he is to be worshipped of men because of his preeminent majesty, and to be appeased for man's own sake because of some imminent necessity.

But what should be so worshipped in accordance with its majesty, and what should be so appeased in behalf of any object, as the supremely good and supremely powerful Spirit, who is Lord of all and who rules all? For, as it is established that through the supreme Good and its supremely wise omnipotence all things were created and live, it is most inconsistent to suppose that the Spirit himself does not rule the beings created by him, or that beings are governed by another less powerful or less good, or by no reason at all, but by the confused flow of events alone. For it is he alone through whom it is well with every creature, and without whom it is well with none, and *from whom*, and *through whom*, and *in whom*, are all things.

Therefore, since he himself alone is not only the beneficent Creator, but the most powerful lord, and most wise ruler of all; it is clear that it is he alone whom every other nature, according to its whole ability, ought to worship in love, and to love in worship; from whom all happiness is to be hoped for; with whom refuge from adversity is to be sought; to whom supplication for all things is to be offered. Truly, therefore, he is not only God, but the only God, ineffably Three and One.

Made in the USA
Columbia, SC
18 May 2022